First World War
and Army of Occupation
War Diary
France, Belgium and Germany

21 DIVISION
62 Infantry Brigade
Queen's (Royal West Surrey Regiment)
3/4th Battalion
1 January 1917 - 31 January 1917

WO95/2156/1

The Naval & Military Press Ltd
www.nmarchive.com
Published in association with The National Archives

Published by

The Naval & Military Press Ltd

Unit 10 Ridgewood Industrial Park,

Uckfield, East Sussex,

TN22 5QE England

Tel: +44 (0) 1825 749494

www.naval-military-press.com

www.nmarchive.com

This diary has been reprinted in facsimile from the original. Any imperfections are inevitably reproduced and the quality may fall short of modern type and cartographic standards.

© **Crown Copyright**
Images reproduced by permission of The National Archives, London, England, 2015.

Contents

Document type	Place/Title	Date From	Date To
Heading	WO95/2156-1		
Heading	3-4th Bn (Queen's) West Surrey Regt 1917 May-1917 Dec		
Heading	War Diary of 3/4 73rd Queens R.W.S. Regt From 30 May 1917 To 30 June 1917 (Volume 1)		
War Diary	Westbere (Kent)	30/05/1917	30/05/1917
War Diary	Southampton	31/05/1917	31/05/1917
War Diary	Havre	01/06/1917	02/06/1917
War Diary	La Loge	03/06/1917	06/06/1917
War Diary	Etrun	07/06/1917	18/06/1917
War Diary	In The Line	19/06/1917	26/06/1917
War Diary	Arras	27/06/1917	30/06/1917
Miscellaneous	3/4th Bn "The Queen's" (R.W.S.) Regt.		
Miscellaneous	10th Brigade.	14/06/1917	14/06/1917
Miscellaneous	4th Division 3904/113	16/06/1917	16/06/1917
Miscellaneous	1st Somerset Light Infantry	17/06/1917	17/06/1917
Miscellaneous	1st Somerset Light Infantry	18/06/1917	18/06/1917
Heading	War Diary Of 3/4 Bn The Queens Vol 2		
War Diary	Arras	01/07/1917	09/08/1917
War Diary	Moyenneville	10/08/1917	17/08/1917
War Diary	Croisilles	18/08/1917	22/08/1917
War Diary	Front Line	23/08/1917	27/08/1917
War Diary	Hamelincourt	28/08/1917	28/08/1917
War Diary	Warlus	29/08/1917	31/08/1917
Miscellaneous	Officer Commanding, 3/4th Bn. "The Queen's" (RWS) Regt.	08/08/1917	08/08/1917
Miscellaneous	O.C., 3/4th Bn. "The Queen's" (RWS) Regt.	03/08/1917	03/08/1917
Operation(al) Order(s)	Operation Order No. 1 by Lt. Col K. A. Oswald Commanding 3/4th Bn. "The Queen's" (RWS) Regiment.	08/08/1917	08/08/1917
Miscellaneous	3/4th "Queen's" (RWS) Regt.	08/08/1917	08/08/1917
Operation(al) Order(s)	Operation Order No. 2 by Lieut. Col. K. A. Oswald Commanding 3/4th Bn. "The Queen's" (RWS) Regiment.	16/08/1917	16/08/1917
Miscellaneous Diagram etc	3/4th Bn. "The Queen's" (RWS). Regiment.	17/08/1917	17/08/1917
Operation(al) Order(s)	Operation Order No 3 by O.C. "Oxen"	21/08/1917	21/08/1917
Miscellaneous	Oxem Provisional Defence Scheme	23/08/1917	23/08/1917
Miscellaneous	Report On Action Of Patrol On Night Of 25/26.8.17		
Operation(al) Order(s)	Operation Order No. 4	26/08/1917	26/08/1917
Operation(al) Order(s)	Operation Order No. 5	27/08/1917	27/08/1917
Miscellaneous	3/4th Bn. "The Queen's" (R.W.S.) Regiment.	01/09/1917	01/09/1917
War Diary	Warlus	01/09/1917	16/09/1917
War Diary	Caestre	17/09/1917	23/09/1917
War Diary	Le Roukloshille	24/09/1917	28/09/1917
War Diary	Reninghelst	29/09/1917	30/09/1917
Miscellaneous	21st. Division Routine Orders. Appendix I	08/09/1917	08/09/1917
Miscellaneous	Corps Routine Orders By Lieutenant General J. A. L. Haldane C. B., D.S.O. Commanding VI Corps. Appendix II	11/09/1917	11/09/1917

Operation(al) Order(s)	Operations Order No. 6 By Lieut. Colonel K.A. Oswald Commanding Oxen. Appendix III	15/09/1917	15/09/1917
Miscellaneous	Administration Instruction No. 1 for Move To 2nd Army Area. Appendix III	15/09/1917	15/09/1917
Operation(al) Order(s)	Operation Order No. 7 by Lieut Colonel K. A. Oswald Commanding "Oxen" Appendix IV	22/09/1917	22/09/1917
Operation(al) Order(s)	Operation Order No. 8 by Lieut. Col. K.A. Oswald Commanding Oxen. Appendix V	28/09/1917	28/09/1917
Miscellaneous	Administration Order No. 1 in conjunction with O.O. No. 8 Appendix V		
Operation(al) Order(s)	Operation Order No. 9 by Lieut. Col. K. A. Oswald Commanding Oxen Appendix VI	30/09/1917	30/09/1917
Heading	3/4 Queens R W Surrey's October 1917		
Map			
War Diary	Zillebeke	01/10/1917	02/10/1917
War Diary	Trenches S. E. of Polygon Wood	03/10/1917	06/10/1917
War Diary	Trenches East Of Polygon Wood	07/10/1917	08/10/1917
War Diary	Zillibeke	09/10/1917	09/10/1917
War Diary	Sercus	10/10/1917	20/10/1917
War Diary	Micmac Camp W Of Dickebusch	21/10/1917	21/10/1917
War Diary	Camp near Kruisstrathoek	22/10/1917	22/10/1917
War Diary	Trenches On Reutel Ridge East Of Polygon Wood	23/10/1917	26/10/1917
War Diary	Zillibeke Lake	27/10/1917	30/10/1917
War Diary	Camp 'C' East of Dickebusch	31/10/1917	31/10/1917
Miscellaneous	No. 202312 Private Charles James Baker 3/4th Bn. "The Queen's" (R.W.S.) Regt. Appendix 21		
Miscellaneous	No. 205735 Private Albert Dix, 3/4th Bn. "The Queen's" (R.W.S.) Regt.		
Miscellaneous	No. 201348 Sergeant Albert Victor Glaze 3/4th Bn. "The Queen's" (R.W.S) Regt.		
Miscellaneous	No. 201584 Private (L/Corporal) Charles Cecil Clark 3/4th Bn. "The Queen's" (R.W.S.) Regt.		
Miscellaneous	No. 20550 Private John Capp. 3/4th Bn. "The Queen's" (R.W.S.) Regt.		
Miscellaneous	No. 205471 Private (L/Corporal) Arthur Victor Lemon, 3/4th Bn. "The Queen's" (R.W.S.) Regt.		
Operation(al) Order(s)	Operation Order No. 9 by Lieut. Col. K. A. Oswald Commanding Oxen Appendix I	02/10/1917	02/10/1917
Operation(al) Order(s)	Operation Order No. 10 By Lieut-Colonel K. A. Oswald Commanding 3/4th Bn. "The Queen's" (RWS) Regt. Appendix 2	02/10/1917	02/10/1917
Operation(al) Order(s)	Operation Order No. 17 by Major H.C. Cannon M.C., Commanding Oxen Appendix 22	28/10/1917	28/10/1917
Miscellaneous	Copy Of Xth Corps Routine Order No. 1834 Appendix 23	29/10/1917	29/10/1917
Miscellaneous	Appendix 8		
Miscellaneous	Captain Mazzini Tron M.C., C.F. att. 3/4th "Queen's" (R.W.S.) Regiment Appendix 24		
Miscellaneous	Report On Machine Guns Appendix 1		
Operation(al) Order(s)	Operation Order No. 11 By Captain V. F. Samuelson Commanding "Oxen" In Front Line. Appendix 4	07/10/1917	07/10/1917
Miscellaneous	Appendix 5	05/10/1917	05/10/1917
Miscellaneous	Appendix 6	10/10/1917	10/10/1917
Miscellaneous	3/4th Bn. "The Queen's" (RWS) Reg Appendix 7		
Miscellaneous	3/4th Bn. "The Queen's" (R.W.S.) Regt. Appendix 9		
Miscellaneous	Incidents Appendix 10		

Operation(al) Order(s)	Operation Order No. 12 By Major H. C. Cannon. M.C. Commanding 3/4th. Bn. "The Queens" (RWS) Regt. Appendix 11	08/10/1917	08/10/1917
Miscellaneous	Administrative Orders.	08/10/1917	08/10/1917
Miscellaneous	3/4th Bn. "The Queen's" (R.W.S.) Regiment Appendix 12		
Operation(al) Order(s)	Operation Order No. 13 By Major M.C. Cannon. M.C., Commanding Oxen. Appendix 13	19/10/1917	19/10/1917
Miscellaneous	Administrative Orders Issued In Conjunction With Operation Order No. 13	19/10/1917	19/10/1917
Operation(al) Order(s)	Operation Order No. 14 by Major H. C. Cannon., M.C. Commanding Oxen Appendix 14	21/10/1917	21/10/1917
Miscellaneous	Amendment To Operation Order No. 14 by Major H. C. Cannon M.C. Commanding Oxen	21/10/1917	21/10/1917
Miscellaneous	Defence Scheme for Battalion Holding left of Left Sub-Sector. Appendix 15		
Map			
Miscellaneous	Relief Orders By Major H.C. Cannon M.C. Commanding Oxen. Appendix 17	24/10/1917	24/10/1917
Miscellaneous	Relief Orders By Major H.C. Cannon M.C. Commanding Oxen. Appendix 18	25/10/1917	25/10/1917
Miscellaneous	O.C. "A" Coy., Oxen Appendix 19	27/10/1917	27/10/1917
Miscellaneous	Extract from Xth Corps Routine Order No. 1826 Appendix 20	27/10/1917	27/10/1917
Heading	War Diary of the 3/4th Bn "The Queen's" (R.W.S.) Regt from 1st November 1917 to 30th November 1917		
War Diary	Camp "C" East of Dicke Busch	01/11/1917	04/11/1917
War Diary	Trenches around Reutel	05/11/1917	08/11/1917
War Diary	Railway Dugouts Zillibeke	09/11/1917	11/11/1917
War Diary	Micmac Camp. West Of Dicke Busch	12/11/1917	15/11/1917
War Diary	Kendra Camp N.E of Westoutre	16/11/1917	17/11/1917
War Diary	Oultersteen	18/11/1917	18/11/1917
War Diary	Oblinghem	19/11/1917	19/11/1917
War Diary	Barlin	20/11/1917	20/11/1917
War Diary	Mount. St. Eloy	21/11/1917	21/11/1917
War Diary	Aubrey Camp S of Ecurie	22/11/1917	30/11/1917
Miscellaneous	3/4th Bn. "The Queen's" (R.W.S.) Regt. Appendix 1	31/10/1917	31/10/1917
Operation(al) Order(s)	Operation Order No. 18 by Major M.C. Cannon, M.C. Commanding Oxen. Appendix 2	03/11/1917	03/11/1917
Map	Appendix 3	08/11/1917	08/11/1917
Miscellaneous	Defence Scheme For Oxen Appendix 4	05/11/1917	05/11/1917
Miscellaneous	Brigade Orders by Brigadier-General G.H. Gater, D.S.O., Commanding 62nd Infantry Brigade. Appendix 5	06/11/1917	06/11/1917
Operation(al) Order(s)	Operation Order No. 19 by Major H.C. Cannon, M.C., Commanding Oxen. Appendix 6	07/11/1917	07/11/1917
Operation(al) Order(s)	Operation Order No. 20 by Major H.C. Cannon, M.C., Commanding Oxen. Appendix 6	11/11/1917	11/11/1917
Miscellaneous	Extract From Xth Corps Routine Orders By Lieut-General Sir. T. L. N. Morland, K.C.B., K.C.M.G., D.S.O. Appendix 8	12/11/1917	12/11/1917
Operation(al) Order(s)	Operation Order No. 21 By Major M.C. Cannon M.C. Commanding Oxen Appendix 9	13/11/1917	13/11/1917
Miscellaneous	G. C. C. and all Ranks, 21st Division Appendix 10	17/11/1917	17/11/1917

Type	Description	Date From	Date To
Operation(al) Order(s)	Operation Order No. 22 by Major M.C. Cannon, M.C., Commanding 3/4th Bn. "The Queen's" (RWS) Rgt. Appendix 11	16/11/1917	16/11/1917
Operation(al) Order(s)	Operation Order No. 23 by Major M.C. Cannon, M.C., Commanding 3/4th Bn. "The Queen's" (RWS) Rgt Appendix 12	17/11/1917	17/11/1917
Operation(al) Order(s)	Operation Order No. 24 by Major H.C. Cannon, M.C. Oxen. Appendix. 13	18/11/1917	18/11/1917
Operation(al) Order(s)	Operation Order No. 25 by Major M.C. Cannon. M.C, Commanding 3/4th Bn. "The Queen's" (RWS) Regt. Appendix 14	19/11/1917	19/11/1917
Operation(al) Order(s)	Operation Order No. 26 by Major H.C. Cannon, M.C. Appendix 15	20/11/1917	20/11/1917
Miscellaneous	Brigade Orders by Brigadier-General C.H. Gater, D.S.O., Commanding 62nd Infantry Brigade. Appendix 16	22/11/1917	22/11/1917
Miscellaneous	3/4th Bn. "Queen's" (RWS) Regt. Instructions. No.1 Appendix 17	24/11/1917	24/11/1917
Miscellaneous	Appendix 18	19/11/1917	19/11/1917
Miscellaneous	Extract From Regimental Orders, Dated 29th Nov/17 Appendix 19	29/11/1917	29/11/1917
War Diary	Mardeuil	01/12/1917	01/12/1917
War Diary	Brusle	02/12/1917	03/12/1917
War Diary	Longavesnes	04/12/1917	09/12/1917
War Diary	Trenches around Vaucelette Farm S. of Gouzeacourt	10/12/1917	15/12/1917
War Diary	Railway Embankment Dugouts	16/12/1917	17/12/1917
War Diary	Heudecourt	18/12/1917	26/12/1917
War Diary	Trenches around Vaucelette Farm S of Gouzeacourt	27/12/1917	31/12/1917
Operation(al) Order(s)	Operation Order No. 29 By Lt Col G. H. Sawyer, D.S.O., Commanding 3/4th Bn "The Queen's" (RWS) Regt. Appendix 1	08/12/1917	08/12/1917
Miscellaneous	Defence Scheme, 3/4th "Queen's" Appendix 3	10/12/1917	10/12/1917
Operation(al) Order(s)	Operation Order No. 30. By Lt. Col. G.H. Sawyer, D.S.O. Commanding "Oxen" Appendix 4	12/12/1917	12/12/1917
Operation(al) Order(s)	Operation Order No. 30. By Lt. Col. G.H. Sawyer, D.S.O. Commanding "Oxen" Appendix 5	14/12/1917	14/12/1917
Operation(al) Order(s)	Operation Order No. 31 3/4th The Queen's R.W.S. Reg. Appendix 6	16/12/1917	16/12/1917
Miscellaneous	Copy of Regimental Order, Dated 25th Decr, 1917. Appendix 7		
Operation(al) Order(s)	Operation Order, No 33 by Lt-Colonel G.H. Sawyer, D.S.O., Commanding 3/4th Bn "The Queen's" (RWS) Regt. Appendix 8	24/12/1917	24/12/1917
Operation(al) Order(s)	3/4th Bn. "The Queen's" (RWS) Regt. Order No. 34 Appendix 9	30/12/1917	30/12/1917
War Diary	Heudecourt	01/01/1917	04/01/1917
War Diary	Trenches around Vaucelette Farm S of Gouzeacourt	05/01/1917	08/01/1917
War Diary	Railway Embankment East of Gouzeacourt	09/01/1917	16/01/1917
War Diary	Heudicourt	17/01/1917	20/01/1917
War Diary	Trenches around Vaucelette Farm S of Gouzeacourt	21/01/1917	24/01/1917
War Diary	Railway Embankment E of Heudicourt	25/01/1917	30/01/1917
War Diary	Moislains	31/01/1917	31/01/1917
Map			
Operation(al) Order(s)	3/4th Bn "The Queen's" (RWS) Regt. Order No. 35 Appendix 1	03/01/1918	03/01/1918

Operation(al) Order(s)	3/4th Bn "The Queen's" (RWS) Regt. Operation Order No 35. Appendix 3	07/01/1918	07/01/1918
Operation(al) Order(s)	3/4th Bn "The Queen's" (RWS) Regt. Operation Order No 36. Appendix 4	11/01/1918	11/01/1918
Operation(al) Order(s)	3/4th Bn "The Queen's" (RWS) Regt. Operation Order No 38. Appendix 5	15/01/1918	15/01/1918
Operation(al) Order(s)	3/4th Bn "The Queen's" (RWS) Regt. Operation Order No 39. Appendix 6	19/01/1918	19/01/1918
Operation(al) Order(s)	Regt Operation Order No. 39		
Operation(al) Order(s)	3/4th Bn "The Queen's" (RWS) Regt. Operation Orders No. 40. Appendix 7	23/01/1918	23/01/1918
Operation(al) Order(s)	3/4th Bn "The Queen's" (RWS) Regt. Operation Orders No. 41. Appendix 8	27/01/1918	27/01/1918
Operation(al) Order(s)	3/4th Bn "The Queen's" (RWS) Regt. Operation Orders No. 42. Appendix 9	30/01/1918	30/01/1918

W0095 2156 11

21ST DIVISION
62ND INFY BDE

3-4TH BN (QUEEN'S)
WEST SURREY REGT
~~AUG 1917 DEC 1917~~

1917 MAY – 1917 DEC

FROM UK

DISBANDED 10.2.1918

Confidential

War Diary
of
3/4 "B" The Queen's R.W.S. Regt.
from 30 May 1917.   to   20 June 1917

(Volume 1)

Attached South African Bde

Army Form C. 2118

3/4 Batt "The Queens"
R.W. Surrey Regt

WAR DIARY
or
INTELLIGENCE SUMMARY
(Erase heading not required.)

Instructions regarding War Diaries and Intelligence Summaries are contained in F.S. Regs., Part II and the Staff Manual respectively. Title Pages will be prepared in manuscript.

Place	Date 1917	Hour	Summary of Events and Information	Remarks and references to Appendices
WESTBERE (KENT)	MAY 30	7 p.m.	Battalion left Camp in 2 equal portions under Lt Col Stooks and Major KP Gosworth entraining at CANTERBURY WEST at 9.40 & 11.40 respectively. A & B Coys in 1st train	W⁰ "Appx I"
SOUTHAMPTON	31	3.20 a.m.	C & D Coys in 2nd Train – Arrived at SOUTHAMPTON Docks Sta at 3.30 & 5.30 am – remained in Sheds during day and embarked on Transport "La MARGUERITE" with 3/4 R.W. Kent Regt at 4 p.m. and sailed at 6 p.m. Strength 1006 including 33 Officers. Nominal Roll attached	W⁰ "Appx I"
HAVRE	JUNE 1	3 am	Arrived in harbour – disembarked 7.30 a.m. – marched to No1 Rest Camp, arrived 10 am – no kit – weather still hot	W⁰
"	2	9.30 a.m.	Left Rest Camp and entrained at Gare de Marchandise HAVRE left 2pm. Short stops at BOUCITY and ABBEVILLE.	W⁰
LA LOGE	3	7.30 a.m.	detrained at HESDIN and proceeded by Road to village of LA LOGE about 5 miles – weather very hot (Men billeted in Barns etc but majority bivouacs in adjoining orchards)	W⁰
"	4		Very hot Route March via FRESSIN.	W⁰
"	5		Training in FOREST D'HESDIN – Transport left 12.30 p.m. for DUISANS – billets near ST POL for night	W⁰
"	6	7 a.m.	Left LA LOGE in 2 portions at 7 & 8 am and Trains left HESDIN at 10 and 11 am for DUISANS – arrived at 2.30 and marched outside STATION till 6 p.m. – Proceeded to Y huts ETRUN. Transport arrived 7.30 p.m. Attached 3rd Army – 17" Corps. 9" Division – S.African Inf. Brigade	W⁰

WAR DIARY
INTELLIGENCE SUMMARY
(Erase heading not required.)

Army Form C. 2118

Place	Date	Hour	Summary of Events and Information	Remarks and references to Appendices
ETRUN	1917 JUNE 7th	8 A.M.	TRAINING	N.P.
"	9th	9 a.m.	Inspection of Battalion by Corps Commander (Sir Chas Fergusson), 9th Divisional Commander (Maj Gen. Lukin) and Brigade Commander (Bg. Gen. F.S. Dawson). Inspection in its field afterwards by Brigadier - rewhite lot.	N.P.
"	10th & 17th		TRAINING during this period the following training was carried out - Range, Field work - attack practice - from Platoons - Live Bombing. Tactical Exercises - Lectures. The Battalion Choir went of Tactical Training and made considerable improvement during its period - on the 11th a Rifle Grenade accident occurred causing 1st a premature - injuring 7 N.C.O's + men of D Coy	N.P.
"	15th	4 p.m.	2 Lt Capt Starke Capt Connacher - 4 Coy Concussion 2nd + Subalterns left Y huts by lorry to visit Front line - attached to 11 B'gde in FAMPOUX sector	N.P.
"	16th	4 p.m.	Maj A.K.H. Ormsby – Lieut Bannerman, Asst Adj, 4 Coy 2nds in Command & 4 Subalterns left Y huts by lorry for instruction in front line - aut at 11.35 p.m.	N.P.
"		12 pm M.N.	1st party returned.	N.P.
"	17th	4 pm	2nd party returned. Concert for men on Parade Ground.	N.P.

WAR DIARY
INTELLIGENCE SUMMARY
(Erase heading not required.)

Army Form C. 2118

Place	Date	Hour	Summary of Events and Information	Remarks and references to Appendices
ETRUN	JUNE 1917 18th	4 p.m.	HQ and 1/2 Battalion left Y huts - 6 p.m. 1/2 Battalion + m. transport lorries came disembarked at ST NICHOLAS. Battalion marched to meet of 1/2 Bn in the line - Transport lines established at CANDLE FACTORY - ST NICHOLAS -	APPX II
		6 p.m.	met by guides at "Blue line" (Ry Bridge H14.a.04 Sh51B) proceeded to Front line sector grid N + S of river SCARPE. Bn HQ officers attached to Bn HQ of units of 11th Bgde + 12th Bgde.	
			A Coy to 1st Som.L.Iny. ⎫ 11 Bgde on Right ⎬ B " 1st Hants Rgt ⎭	W.O.
			C " " 1st Lanc's Fus ⎫ 12 Bgde on Left ⎬ D " " 1st Essex Rgt ⎭	W.O.
IN THE LINE	19th to 26th		Instruction in Trench warfare - see appendix.	
"	21st	4 p.m.	Lieut Col Lt. Hooke, the CO, killed near Chemical works (nr Pt H18.d.3.6 sheet 51 B) while going from Reserve to Front line with a small party of 'C' Coy. A shell burst in the parapet wounding the CO in the head and Lt F.W.A Brecker in thigh, also Pte Smith the CO's Batman, after attending to the CO Lieut Brecker proceeded with his party to the front line being compelled to return to Quarry station later. Lt Col Hooke was taken to Adv Dressing Station at PAMPOUX lock when he died some 5 mins after arrival. never having regained consciousness. He was buried in the military cemetery at Pt H2.3 B7.5. not far from the place where he was hit at 9.45 p.m. - Rev Waldegrave C.F. 10th Bde officiated. -	W.O.

Army Form C. 2118

WAR DIARY
INTELLIGENCE SUMMARY
(Erase heading not required.)

Place	Date	Hour	Summary of Events and Information	Remarks and references to Appendices
IN THE LINE	JUNE 1917 22"		Major K.A. Oswald assumed Temporary Command of the Battalion	N.T.O
"	26"	10.pm	"B" "C" "D" Coys out of line and embussed at Blue line Ry Bridge. H'y.a.o.s.	N.T.O
ARRAS	27"	1.30 am	— do — arrived in ARRAS and billetted in OIL FACTORY (Place St Croix). Officers billetted in house near	
		10 pm	"A" Coy came out of front line -	N.T.O
"	28"	2 am	"A" Coy arrived at OIL FACTORY. Casualties during attachment in line were Officers - Killed 1 - wounded 1 - Other Ranks killed 12 - wounded 36 - The Battalion did some cleaning, a rather trying period. Shell fire was almost continuous. The men were steady and always cheerful. There was difficulty in the distribution of Rations over so wide a front, but the Q.M's & Transport department did very satisfactory work. The Brigade Commander and O.C. units to which Battalion was attached expressed satisfaction at the work and conduct of the Battalion -	N.T.O
"	29"		"B" & "B" Coys at the disposal of C.R.E. 4" Div. for work	
			"C" " " 6" " " " "	
			"D" " " 11" " " " "	
			Meeting held 6" & 12" Divisions in Arras - commenced by Lt Col Ross formerly an Officer of this Battalion	
Attacked	30"	10 am	"C" & "D" Coys move to horse exton Camp in West of 1"3 huline "(H.14.a.o.8.) - "C" by in Ry Cutting - "D" in ground just WEST of it. Strength of Battalion 9S'2 including Maj. Whitney and the command of Maj's Whitney. Strength of Battalion 9.5.2 including 31 Officers.	N.T.O

3/4th Bn "THE QUEEN'S" (R.W.S.) Regt.

Rank	Name	Disposal	Date of Substantive Rank and Rank		Date of Acting Rank.
A/Lieut Col	U.L.Hooke	C.O.	6/7/10	Major	15/5/15
Major	K.A.Oswald,	2nd in Comm'd	1/6/16	Major	
A/Major	F.T.Whinney,	Comm'g "C" Co	-do-	Captain	5/5/17
Captain	A.H.Harper,	Comm'g "D" Co	-do-	-do-	
A/Captain	A.T.Latham,	.. "B" Co	-do-	Lieut	
A/Captain	P.M.Hepworth,	.. "A" Co	-do-	-do-	-do-
A/Captain & Adjutant	V.F.Samuelson,	Adjutant,	-do-	-do-	-do-
Lieutenant	L.J.C.Vidler,	"A" Co	-do-	-do-	
A/Captain	C.G.Moss,	"B" Co	-do-	-do-	-do-
A/Captain	G.A.Ionides,	"C" Co	-do-	-do-	-do-
Lieutenant	E.W.Preston,	Transport Officer.	-do-	-do-	
Lieut & Q.M.	T.I.Birch,	QuarterMaster	26/4/15	-do-	
A/Lieutentant	H.P.McCabe,	"D" Co	1/6/16	2nd Lieut	-do-
A/Lieutenant	H.W.Carter,	Signal Officer	-do-	-do-	-do-
A/Lieutenant	A.B.Frost,	"B" Co	-do-	-do-	-do-
A/Lieutenant	F.W.A.Buckell	"C" Co	-do-	-do-	-do-
A/Lieutenant	R.R.B.Bannerman,	Assistant Adjt & L.G. Officer	-do-	-do-	-do-
A/Lieutenant	G.A.Shaw,	"D" Co	-do-	-do-	-do-
A/Lieutenant	A.H.A.Cooper,	"C" Co	-do-	-do-	-do-
2nd Lieut	J.Ost, XX	"B" Co	4/11/16	-do- XX	
-do-	W.A.Puddicombe,	"C" Co	20/3/15	-do-	
-do-	A.H.Lovell,	"A" Co	10/10/15	-do-	
-do-	E.H.Dakin,	"D" Co	-do-	-do-	
-do-	D.R.J.O'Connor,	"D" Co	-do-	-do-	
-do-	A.H.John,	Scout & Sniping Officer,	-do-	-do-	
-do-	H.E.Fisk,	"A" Co	22/10/15	-do-	
-do-	W.P.Thomas,	"A" Co	28/10/15	-do-	
-do-	A.E.Barrow,	"B" Co	28/11/15	-do-	
-do-	J.R.Skeet,	"B" Co	20/12/15	-do-	
-do-	H.S.Gilliland,	Battalion Bombing Officer	16/4/16	-do-	
-do-	J.C.Davie,	"A" Co	28/2/17	-do-	
-do-	C.A.Freestone,	"C" Co	1/3/17	-do-	
Captain	A.E.Mackenzie,	R.A.M.C.	T.Attached		

XX Retains seniority from 13/11/14. (London Gazette 6/5/17).

4th Div. G.S. 9/40.

10th Brigade.
11th Brigade.
12th Brigade.
South African Brigade)
9th Div. Q.   ) for information.
4th Div. Q.
----

1. The 3rd/4th Queens (R.W.S.) Regt. will be attached to the Division from the 18th instant for instruction in trench warfare.
    'A' and 'B' Companies will be attached to the Right Brigade, 'C' and 'D' Companies to the Left Brigade in the line.
    Each of the above Companies should be attached to one of the battalions actually holding the line.
    Battalion Headquarters will be attached to Brigade Headquarters Right Brigade.

2. Training should be carried out on the following lines -

   (a) Officers and N.C.Os. to be attached to units in the line corresponding to those they command for a period, including the carrying out of a relief. Special attention to be paid to instruction in the method of taking over trenches, bringing up rations etc., and trench routine.

   (b) Complete platoons to be attached to companies in the line for one complete period in the trenches including the relief.

   (c) Complete companies to be attached to Battalions for one complete tour of duty.

3. The battalion will move on the 18th so as to be at Railway Bridge H.14 a 0.4 at 9 p.m. where it will be met by guides from Brigades concerned.

4. Orders re move from Y Huts to rendezvous, disposal of transport, rationing, will be issued by 4th Div. Q.

5. Two officers from each Company will be attached to Battalions on 15th/16th June and two more on 16th/17th. Two Officers from Battalion Headquarters will be attached to Brigade Headquarters Right Brigade for the same periods. Arrangements for transport will be made by 4th Div. Q.

14th June, 1917.

W.Kirke, Colonel,
General Staff, 4th Division.

Copies to 9th Div. G.   )
         3/4th Queens (R.W.S.)R.) for information.
         XVII Corps   )

4th Division 3904/113.

South African Brigade.
10th Brigade.
11th Brigade.
12th Brigade.
9th Division "Q"
4th Division "G"
Area Commdt. BLANGY,
A.P.M. 4th Division,
3/4 Queen's (R.W.S.) Regt.)   for information.
XVIIth Corps.   )
----

1.   Reference 4th Division G.S. 9/40 of 14/6/17 re move of 3/4 (Queen's) West Surrey Regt.

        Lorries to carry 500 all ranks will report at "Y" Huts at 4 p.m. 18th instant, and will convey party to ST NICHOLAS Church (G 16 c 5.7).
        After off loading the 1st party about 5 p.m. the Lorries will return to "Y" Huts and bring the remainder of the Battalion to St. NICHOLAS Church arriving there about 7 p.m.

2.   The Battalion will move by march route from ST NICHOLAS to the Bridge under Railway Embankment at H 14 a 0.4, where guides from the 11th and 12th Infantry Brigades will meet the Companies.

3.   The 1st Party to consist of H.Q. and C and D Companies. The 2nd Party of A and B Companies.

4.   The Battalion will march by Half Companies with intervals of 200 yards between Half Companies.

5.   The Route will be by the Main ST NICHOLAS - ST LAURENT BLANGY - FAMPOUX Road.

6.   The A.P.M. 4th Division will arrange for a guide for the leading Half Company of each party.

7.   The leading Half Company will arrive at Railway Embankment about 6 p.m., when it will come under orders of 12th Brigade.
        The leading Half Company of A and B Companies will arrive at Railway Embankment about 8.15 p.m. and will come under orders of 11th Brigade.

8.   The 9th Division will continue to ration the Battalion.

9.   Transport Lines near the CANDLE FACTORY (G 16 b 8.2) will be allotted by Area Commandant BLANGY Area to whom a representative of Battalion will report at 9 a.m. 17th instant.

10.   11th and 12th Brigades will arrange for a limber carrying the Companies rations to be picked up by each of the battalions in the line from the Queen's Transport each day.

11.   The Transport will move by march route via main ARRAS - ST POL Road and St. NICHOLAS so as to have time to settle into their lines before night-fall.

                                G.H.MARTIN, Lieut.Colonel,
16/6/17.   A.A. & Q.M.G. 4th Division.

11th Infantry Brigade No.B.M.73/416.

1st Somerset Light Infantry.
1st East Lancashire Regiment.
1st Hampshire Regiment.
1st Rifle Brigade.
Staff Captain.
Brigade Signalling Officer.
3/4th Queen's" (RWS)Regt.
Brigade Transport Officer.

Reference 11th Brigade B.M. 73/344 of the 15th June.
----

(1). Battalion Headquarters of the 3/4th Queens will be attached to Brigade and Battalion Headquarters as follows:-

    Commanding Officer.   )
    Bombing Officer.   )   1st Hampshire Regiment.
    Medical Officer.   )

    Second in Command.   )
    Adjutant.   )   1st Somerset Light Infantry.

    Lewis Gun Officer   )
    Intelligence Officer)   1st East Lancashire Regiment.
    Battalion Gas N.C.O.)

    Signalling Officer)
    1 Sergeant   )   )
    1 Corporal   )Signa-)   Brigade Headquarters.
    4 Other Ranks)llers)

The remainder of Battalion Headquarters will remain with the 1st Line transport of the 3/4th Queens.
The Officers attached to 1st Hampshire Regiment, and 1st East Lancashire Regiment will remain with those regiments on relief thus allowing all Officers to have experience in the trenches.
On the relief of the 1st Somerset Light Infantry by the 1st Rifle Brigade the Second in Command and Adjutant of the 3/4th Queens will be attached to the 1st Rifle Brigade.
Battalions will arrange to send guides for the Officers of Battalion H.Q. attached to them, to be at the railway arch H.14 a.0.4. at 6 p.m. on the 18th inst. in addition to those detailed for Companies, which will be there at 9p.m.
A & B Companies 3/4th Queens Regt. will arrive at the railway arch about 8.15 p.m. where they will halt and bivouac on the South of the ARRAS - FAMPOUX road (West of the Railway Arch) till 9 p.m. at which time the leading platoon of B Company will move off.

                                                   (Sgd.) F.W.Hanton,
                                                         Captain,
                                                     Brigade Major
17th June 1917.   11th Infantry Brigade.

11th Brigade No. B.M.73/465.

1st Somerset Light Infantry.
1st East Lancashire Regiment.
1st Hampshire Regiment.
1st Rifle Brigade.
3/4th Queen's (R.W.S.) Regt.

The B.G.C. wishes the training of the 3/4th Queen's (R.W.S.) Regiment to be carried out as follows:-
(1). For the 1st three days 1 platoon of each Company of the Queens will be attached to each Company of the Battalion in the subsector concerned. During this period the men of the platoon will be distributed throughout the Company, so that they can receive individual instruction.
(2). For the next two days 1 platoon of each Company of the Queens R.W.S. Regt. will be attached to each Company of the Battalion concerned as a complete Unit.
N.B. During these first 5 days the personnel of the Queens will be under the Command of the Platoon or Company Commander to which they are attached.
(3). For the next two days each Company of the Queens will hold a Company front as a complete Unit.
(4). On the last day the Company of the Queens in the case of each subsector will be withdrawn to support or reserve.

PROGRAMME.

June.
18/19th)
19/20th) 1 platoon of 3/4th Queens to each Company of the Battalions
20/21st) in the Line for individual instruction.

21/22nd) 1 platoon of 3/4th Queens to be attached to each Company
22/23rd) of the Battalion in the Line as a complete Unit.

23/24th) 1 Company of the 3/4th Queens to hold a company front as
24/25th) a complete unit, under the Command of the O.C.Subsector.

25/26th) 1 Company of 3/4th Queens in Support or reserve to Battalions of the 11th Brigade holding the line.

3/4th Queens R.W.S.Regt. will remain in the line throughout this period attached to the Battalions of the 11th Brigade in the line.

(Sgd.) F. W. Hanton,
Captain,
Brigade Major.
11th Infantry Brigade.

18th June 1917..

War Diary

of

3/4 Bn

The Queens

Transferred to 62 Bde
8.17.   71

Army Form C. 2118

WAR DIARY
or
INTELLIGENCE SUMMARY
(Erase heading not required.)

[Stamp: 2/4th BATTALION QUEEN'S R. WEST SURREY REGT. No. A/363 Date 1/8/17]

Place	Date 1917	Hour	Summary of Events and Information	Remarks and references to Appendices
ARRAS	July 1st to 6th		Strength of Battalion 943 including 31 Officers.	W.O.
"	8th		"A" + "B" Coys digging by night on MUSKET & CUSP Trenches (S.I.B. I 31.c.) ("D" I 19.c.)	W.O.
"	9th		"C" + "D" " " " "day in vicinity of GAVRELLE SWITCH (" I.1.a)	W.O.
"	9th to 12th		"C" + "D" Coys under orders of C.E. XVII Corps remained quartered in hutting in BLUE LINE (H.14.a.0.8) "A"B"C" + "D" Coys continued working from ARRAS (by light Railway) + BLUE LINE	W.O.
"	13th	noon	Whole Battalion concentrated in ARRAS - attacked for work to 12th Divn.	W.O.
"	14th to 18th		Whole Battalion at work by night in MONCHY - CAMBRAI ROAD Sectors - digging + shell carrying for T.M.Bs.	W.O.
"	20th		"A" "B" + "C" Coys provided detachment of 312 for work under C.R.E. 12 Divn in neighbourhood of MONCHY. They were quartered in Chessed trenches and dugouts in old BROWN LINE (S.I.B. N.10.c.7.7.) Detacht. under command of Major F. Whinney.	
"	21st		Capt. A. T. Lotham took over command of Detachment in BROWN LINE.	W.O.
"	23rd		Attachment to 9th Division ceased. Battalion attached for Administration and Training to 12th Division in ARRAS.	W.O.

Army Form C. 2118

WAR DIARY
or
INTELLIGENCE SUMMARY
(Erase heading not required.)

Instructions regarding War Diaries and Intelligence Summaries are contained in F. S. Regs., Part II. and the Staff Manual respectively. Title Pages will be prepared in manuscript.

Place	Date 1917 July	Hour	Summary of Events and Information	Remarks and references to Appendices
ARRAS	27th		Battalion mentioned in report of Maj. Gen. A.B. Scott (Comdg 12 Divn) for good work in digging & carrying out in connection with 12th Divn operation in neighbourhood of LONG TRENCH (MONCHY SECTOR) 15th–17th July 1917.	W.O.
"	23rd to 31st		Working parties provided from ARRAS area. BROWN LINE as previously - Strength of Battalion 31.7.17 - 919 including 31 officers.	W.O.
"	1st to 31st		General - Health of Battalion good - Casualties O.R. 1 killed, wounded 17 wounded. Training was carried out whenever possible - Signallers Lewis Gunners - Battalion Classes for Lewis Gunners & Rifle Bombers - Officers & N.C.O's attended Army - Corps & Divnl Schools.	W.O.

W. Oswald
Lt. Col. "The Queen"
Comdg 3/4 Br R.W.S.R.t.

Army Form C. 2118

WAR DIARY
INTELLIGENCE SUMMARY

3/4th Bn (Queen's) Royal West Surrey Regt

Vol 3

(Erase heading not required.)

Place	Date 1917 August	Hour	Summary of Events and Information	Remarks and references to Appendices
ARRAS	1st		Strength 919 incl 31 Officers – Working and carrying by day and night from ARRAS (D Coy) and from BROWNLINE (A,B & C Coys) – in vicinity of MONCHY.	Nil
"	2nd	10-11 pm	2nd Lieut Pendrigh's stack of strength (S–sea). Working Parties encountered MUSTARD gas in vicinity of CMB & RP1 Road – and FOSSES FM. casualties viz.	APPX I Nil
"	3rd		Weather wet – work as above continued	
"	4th		" " " " " " . Lieut F.M.A. Birkett rejoined – (wounded 21/5/17)	Nil
"	5th		] work continued	Nil
"	6th			Nil
"	7th	4pm	Detachment (HQ & C Coys) returned from BROWN LINE	Nil
"	8th		Battalion at OIL FACTORY. Cleaning up. Letter of appreciation in work done from M.Gen SCOTT. Comng 12th Divn.	APPX II Nil
"	9th	10.30 am	Move to MOYENNEVILLE – arrived 3.15 p.m. Distance 9 miles – marching good – In Camp & huts. "D" Coy in NISSEN huts HAMELINCOURT 600 yards away. Attached 62nd Bgde – 21st Divn – VI Corps. Marching in strength 30 officers. 653 O.R. 55 horses. 22 vehicles – Divisional and Corps Commanders at OIL FACTORY when Bn't left.	APPX III Nil

1875 Wt. W593/826 1,000,000 4/15 J.B.C. & A.   A.D.S.S./Forms/C. 2118.

Army Form C. 2118

WAR DIARY
INTELLIGENCE SUMMARY
(Erase heading not required.)

Instructions regarding War Diaries and Intelligence Summaries are contained in F.S. Regs., Part II. and the Staff Manual respectively. Title Pages will be prepared in manuscript.

Place	Date 1917	Hour	Summary of Events and Information	Remarks and references to Appendices
MOYENNE -VILLE	Aug 10th		In Camp - Cleaning up	N.T.O
"	11th		Divisional Horse Show - Battalion entered in several events - several lst prizes	N.T.O.
"	12th to 15th		} Training	N.T.O
"	16th		Battalion inspected by Divisional Commander (M. Gen. Campbell) & Brigadier (Brig. Gen. Rawling CMG) - C.O. (Lt. Col K.G. Seward) invested Batt'y in Reserve H.Q. (CROISILLES)	N.T.O.
"	17th		Moved to CROISILLES as Battalion in Reserve - practice in changing of shelters - Relief complete 4.20 p.m	APPX No IV
CROISILLES	18th		Improving shelters & dug outs - Reconnoitering Routes to Front lines. Sunk Road Sullied S.B. 7.2.2 & 9.5 near Bn. 159. Two Casualties	N.T.O
"	19th		C.O. Adjutant - Coy Commanders visited Front Line - Left Brigade Sector - Left Subsector - in front of FONTAINE - 1st old HINDENBURG LINE.	N.T.O
"	20th		} Battalion in Reserve - work on shelters etc.	N.T.O
"	21st			N.T.O

WAR DIARY or INTELLIGENCE SUMMARY

Army Form C. 2118

Place	Date	Hour	Summary of Events and Information	Remarks and references to Appendices
CROISILLES	Aug 1917 22		Move to Front Line – Relief of Brigade Sector – relieved 12/13 Northumberland Fusiliers. Transport moved to BOYELLES.	APPX V W/D
FRONT LINE	23rd		Patrols to all parts of No mans land – no sign of enemy – Defence Scheme.	APPX VI W/D
"	24th		Quiet day – Reconnoitering enemy position East of PUG AVENUE	W/D
"	25th		Officers of R. Dublin Fusiliers visit line. Patrol under 2Lt H.S.GILLILAND entered enemy line near PUG AVENUE – 1 Officer & 2 O.R. wounded. Valuable information as to enemy situation obtained.	APPX VII W/D
"	26th		Quiet day	W/D
"	27th	7.30 p.m.	Relief by 6/15 Bn R Dublin Fusiliers – Battalion in huts at HAMELIN– COURT. Very rough weather – Relief delayed, complete 7.30 P.M. Casualties in line – Killed 2 – Wounded, 1 Officer, 11 O.Ranks	APPX VIII W/D
HAMELIN– COURT	28th	10.15 p.m.	Battalion moved to WARLUS for training – Distance 10 miles – arrived 3.30 PM – in Billets own in BARNS.	APPX IX W/D
WARLUS	29th 30th		Cleaning up & 2/1 Divn transferred to XVII Corps from VI Corps.	W/D
"	31st		Training – Strength of Batt 2 Q11 including 41 Officers.	APPX X W/D

V.A.Oswald Lt Col
Comdg 2/4 Queens Regt.

12th Division No. G/1086.

Officer Commanding,
    3/4th Bn. "The Queen's" (RWS)Regt.

At the conclusion of their attachment to the 12th Division, the Major-General Commanding desires to express to Lieut. Colonel K.A.OSWALD and all ranks of the 3/4 Bn. "The Queen's" (R.W.Surrey) Regiment, his appreciation of the good work they have done while under his Command.

Though not of a fighting nature, the work has been most important, and the Battalion can be assured that it will be highly appreciated by those who will profit by it.

Major-General SCOTT wishes them all luck with their new Division.

(Sgd.) R. S. Allen,
Lieut.Colonel,
General Staff,
12th Division.

8th August, 1917.

In the Field,
August, 3rd, 1917.

From:-
    O. C.,
        3/4th Bn. "The Queen's" (RWS)Regt.

To:-
    Headquarters,
        12th Division.

      With reference to notes and instructions recently issued regarding the new "mustard" Gas used by the Germans, I beg to report for your information that Working parties of the Battalion came into contact with the Gas last night (2/3 August) and I have ascertained the following particulars from the Officers in charge:-

1. Time. about 10.30 p.m. onwards.

2. Area. The Gas was encountered in GORDON - PICK and VINE AVENUES and along CAMBRAI ROAD as far as FOSSES FARM.

3. EFFECTS. The Gas was recognised at once by Officers and men. The usual symptons were unmistakeable - smarting of the eyes, sneezing, and a certain burning all over face was felt.

    The smell was expressed as that of "Horse Radish", yellow flames of about 1 minute's duration were seen on ground and yellow fumes were given off.

    The shells were freely mixed with H.E. and Shrapnel. The dull explosion of the Gas shell was clearly discernable, when it could be heard separate from other bursts.

4. Box Respirators. Gave complete protection, they were worn for periods of over 1 hour in most cases.

5. Casualties. Serious, Nil - One Officer and several men slightly affected. The Officer probably owing to removing Respirator from time to time to test atmosphere.

6. Remarks. One Officer reports that while attending to a wounded man on a stretcher in the bottom of a trench he was unable to detect Gas, but on standing up it was very clearly present.

    That there was no serious consequences, I put down to the fact that the Gas was recognised immediately & B.Rs. adjusted quickly.

                      Lieut. Colonel,
        Commanding 3/4th Bn. "The Queen's" (RWS) Regt.

SECRET.

OPERATION ORDER No.1
by Lt.Col.K.A.Oswald
Commanding 3/4th Bn. "The Queen's" (RWS) Regiment.

COPY No. 9

MAP REF: LENS
Sheet 11.

8/8/17.

1. The Battalion will move to MOYENNEVILLE tomorrow 9.8.17 by Route March to join the 21st Division.

2. The Route will be ARRAS - BOIRY ST. RICTRUDE Road.

3. The Battalion will move as follows :-

    H.Q. .... 10.30 a.m.
    "A" Co............ 10.32 a.m.
    "B" " .... 10.38 a.m.
    "C" " .... 10.44 a.m.
    "D" " .... 10.50 a.m.
    Transport.......... 10.55 a.m.

    The corresponding distances will be maintained.
    Headquarters will be composed of H.Q.Signallers, S.O., L.G.O., B.O., Sergt.Major and H.Q.Clerks.
    The Medical Officer and Maltese Cart will move in rear of "D" Co.

4. Rations - Dinners will be served "en route". Officers will carry Haversack Rations. The Officers' Mess Cart will not be available.

5. Dress - Full Marching Order.

6. An advance party consisting of C.Q.M.S (or assistant) of each Coy. and the Scout Section under 2/Lt. A.H.John, will leave the OIL FACTORY at 9.30 a.m. 9.8.17.

7. Guides - O.C.Scouts will detail 5 guides to be at BOIRY Cross Roads at 2.15 p.m. (1 per Coy. and Transport).

8. O.C.Signals will detail 1 N.C.O. and 3 men (from same Coy.) on bicycles to move on ARRAS-BOISLEUX-AU-MONT Road (special instructions will be issued.)

9. The Drums will parade as a separate section and move off with "A" Coy. Valises and rifles to be stacked at Q.M.Stores by 7.30 a.m.

TRANSPORT.   Special instructions have been issued.

WATCHES.   Will be synchronised at H.Q. at 9 a.m. 9.8.17.

REPORTS.   To Head of Column.

Lieut. & Adjutant.
3/4th Bn. "The Queen's" (RWS) Regt.

Issued at 2.30 p.m. by Orderly.

No. 1   Filed.
 " 2/5 O.C.Coys.
 " 6   Q.M.
 " 7   Sig.O.
 " 8   Sct.O.
 " 9/10 War Diary.
 " 11   T.O.
 " 12   M.O.

3/4th "Queen's" (RWS)Regt.   8.8.17.

INSTRUCTIONS FOR MOVEMENT OF BATTALION ISSUED IN CONJUNCTION WITH OPERATION ORDER No. 1 OF THIS DATE.

TRANSPORT.

4 Coy. L.G.Limbers,) Will all be deposited outside the Oil Fact-
2 Tool Limbers,   ) ory in Place St. Croix, drawn up close
3 S.A.A.Limbers,   ) under the walls of the houses by 4 p.m.
Maltese Cart,   ) 8.8.17.
2 Baggage Waggons.)

1 Bomb Limber. .. Half for Grenades, half at disposal of Transport Officer, to be at Oil Factory at 9.30 a.m. tomorrow 9.8.17.

Officers' Mess Cart. To be at Officers' Mess at 9 a.m. 9.8.17.

Water Carts. .. To be at Oil Factory filled ready to move at 10.30 a.m.

HORSES. .. .. Horses for all waggons deposited in Place St. Croix tonight will be at the Oil Factory at 10.15 a.m. 9.8.17.
One pair will be at Oil Factory at 8.30 a.m. 9.8.17 to work with one of the Limbers there; they will not return to the Transport Lines.
Horses for Cookers will be at Oil Factory at 10.15 a.m. 9.8.17.
Officers' Chargers will be at Oil Factory at 10.15 a.m.
Pack Ponies at Oil Factory at 10.15 a.m.

The Transport, less Cookers, Lewis Gun Limbers and Pack Ponies which will move with respective Companies, will be ready to move from the Oil Factory at 10.55 a.m.

WORKING PARTIES.

O.C. "C" Coy. will supply one N.C.O. and four men to load baggage waggons, to report to Quartermaster at 9 a.m. tomorrow 9.8.17.

O.C.Companies will send loaders for Pack Ponies to Oil Factory at 10.15 a.m. Two men per Coy. and one N.C.O. to be detailed by O.C. "D" Coy.

Companies will be responsible for the loading of their own Lewis Gun Limbers tonight.

BREAKFAST.

Breakfast tomorrow, 9.8.17, will be at 6.30 a.m.

SICK PARADE

will be at 8.0 a.m.

BILLETS.

All Officers' billets will be empty, cleaned, and ready for handing over by 10.30 a.m. The Oil Factory and "D" Coy's. billets by 11.0 a.m. The last Refuse Cart will leave Oil Factory at 9.15 a.m.

PARADES.

Companies will move off as ordered in Operation Order No.1.

RATIONS.

Dinners will be served en route. Headquarters, as detailed in Operation Order No. 1, from "A" Co's. Cooker.

Transport (in rear of Battalion, about 25 men) from "D" Co's. Cooker.

Scouts and others in advance party will require a haversack ration.

BAND.

The Band will parade as a separate section, and will play with different Companies on different sections of the route.

V. F. Samuelson
ADJUTANT,
Bn. "THE QUEENS" R.W.S. REGT.

SECRET.   OPERATION ORDER No. 2, by
Lieut.Col. K.A.OSWALD,
Commanding 3/4th Bn."The Queen's" (RWS) Regiment.

Ref:- MAP 51 B,S.W.   Copy No. 6
                                                       16.8.1917.

1. **MOVE.**   The Battalion, less Transport and Details, will move by road tomorrow into Brigade Reserve, relieving the 9th Bn. Leicester Regt. Companies will relieve the correspondingly lettered Company.
The order of moving will be as follows:-
"A" Coy. 12.30 p.m. by platoons at 5 minutes interval.
"B" "   12.50 p.m.   do.   do.   do.
"C" "   1.10 p.m.   do.   do.   do.
"D" "   1.30 p.m.   do.   do.   do.
Battalion Headquarters 1.45 p.m.

Company Hdqtrs. will move with the leading platoon.

2. **ROUTE.**   The route will be as follows - HAMELINCOURT - dry weather track to MAISON ROUGE FM. (300 x South) - ST. LEGER CROSS ROADS - CROISILLES.

3. **GUIDES.**   One Guide per platoon and Bn. Headquarters from Leicester Regt. will be at ST. LEGER CROSS ROADS at 1.45 p.m.

4. **DRESS.**   Field Service Order.

5. **RATIONS.**   Dinners will be served before leaving. Teas after arrival.

6. **ADVANCE PARTY.**   One Officer and one N.C.O. per Coy. and H.Q. will report at Orderly Room at 11 a.m. and proceed direct to take over new quarters.

7. **TRANSPORT.**   Will move to new Transport Lines on 19th inst. under orders issued by Transport Officer.   Special instructions are being issued for Transport work tomorrow.

8. **DETAILS.**   Will move to new Transport Lines on 19th inst. under orders issued by Transport Officer.

9. **RELIEF.**   All Trench Stores - Defence Schemes - aeroplane photographs etc. will be taken over on relief, and O.C. Companies will advise quantities taken over to Battn.Hdqtrs. as soon as possible. Completion of relief will be reported to H.Q. by Codeword " N A C N U D ".

10. **REPORTS.**   xxxxxxxxxxxxxxxxxxxxxxxxxxx   Battn. Headquarters will open at T.22.d.9.5. at 3 p.m. 17th August,

                                       Captain & Adjutant.
                                       3/4th Bn."The Queen's" (RWS) Regt.

Issued by Orderly at
9 a.m. 17.8.17.

Copy No. 1/4 O.C.Coys.
 "   " 5/6 War Diary.
 "   "   7   Q.M.
 "   "   8   Trans.O.
 "   "   9   Hdqtrs.Offs.
 "   " 10   Filed.
 "   " 11   do.
 "   " 12   do.

3/4th Bn. "THE QUEEN'S" (RWS.) REGIMENT.

Instructions for movement of Battalion in conjunction with Operation Order No. 2 of this date.

TRANSPORT.   4 Coy. L.G.Limbers will report respective Coy. Hdqtrs. at 9 a.m. 17th inst: and proceed with Companies, returning Transport Lines on completion of duty.

1 LIMBER.   Report at Guard Room 12 noon to convey Officers' Bags moving with Battalion Hdqtrs. at 1.45 p.m.

1 LIMBER.   Report Sunken Road at 1 p.m. to convey Coy. Mess stores, (rear part of Limber) and Hdqtrs. stores, Orderly Room, (front portion) moving with Battn. Hdqtrs. at 1.45 p.m.

1 TOOL LIMBER.   Report Q.M.Stores by 12 noon to be loaded and proceed with "D" Coy. at 1.30 p.m. from hutments. Tools will be unloaded and kept in charge of O.C. "D" Coy. - they can be issued to Companies for work after 3.30 p.m.

1 LIMBER.   Report Q.M.Stores at 11 a.m. to convey water cans to "D" Coy. Lines - and dump them.

OFFICERS' MESS CART.   Report Officers' Mess by 11 a.m. 17th inst. and proceed with Battn.Hdqtrs. at 1.45 p.m.

WATER CARTS.   Both will be filled with full complement of petrol tins ready to move from Transport Lines, 1 with "B" Co. 12.50 p.m. and 1 with "D" Co. 1.30 p.m.

1 LIMBER.   Report Q.M. 11 a.m. to convey fuel etc., moving with Battn. Hdqtrs. at 1.45 p.m.

MEDICAL OFFICER'S CART.   Report M.O's. tent at 11 a.m. and proceed with Battn. Hdqtrs. at 1.45 p.m.

HORSES.   Coy. Commanders will notify Transport Officer of the hour for their chargers. Grooms will march with Coys.

ALL Transport, except Water Carts, will return to Transport Lines at earliest possible moment.

CAMP.   The Camp will be left scrupulously clean, tent flys will be rolled up weather permitting, and a certificate to that effect rendered to Battn. Headquarters half an hour before each Coy. moves.

OFFICERS' VALISES.   All Officers' valises will be stored under instructions from the Quartermaster.

DINNERS.   Will be served at 11.45 a.m.

TEAS?   After arrival.

ADVANCE PARTIES.   O.C. Coys. will each detail one Officer and one N.C.O. to report to Battn.Hdqtrs. at 11 a.m. to proceed and take over. Lieut. Bannerman and Sgt. Harding (Signallers) will accompany this party representing Battn. Headquarters.

OFFICERS' KITS.   Officers may take a small roll, consisting of Blanket, waterproof etc. which will be deposited at Guard tent by 12 noon, and be conveyed to New Battn.Hdqtrs. to be fetched by respective Officers' Servants any time after 4 p.m.

P.T.O.

SCOUTS.	2nd Lt. J.R.Skeet and the Scout Section will be attached to "D" Coy. for rations and accommodation from tea 17.8.17 inclusive.
STRETCHER BEARERS.	All stretcher bearers will carry rifles, stretchers taken on M.O's. cart.

J. Hamilton
Captain & Adjutant,
3/4th Bn."The Queen's" (R.W.S.) Regiment.

Issued at 9 a.m.
17.8.17.

One copy with each
Operation Order No. 2.

Map of Front Line Posis   Scale 1/10,000

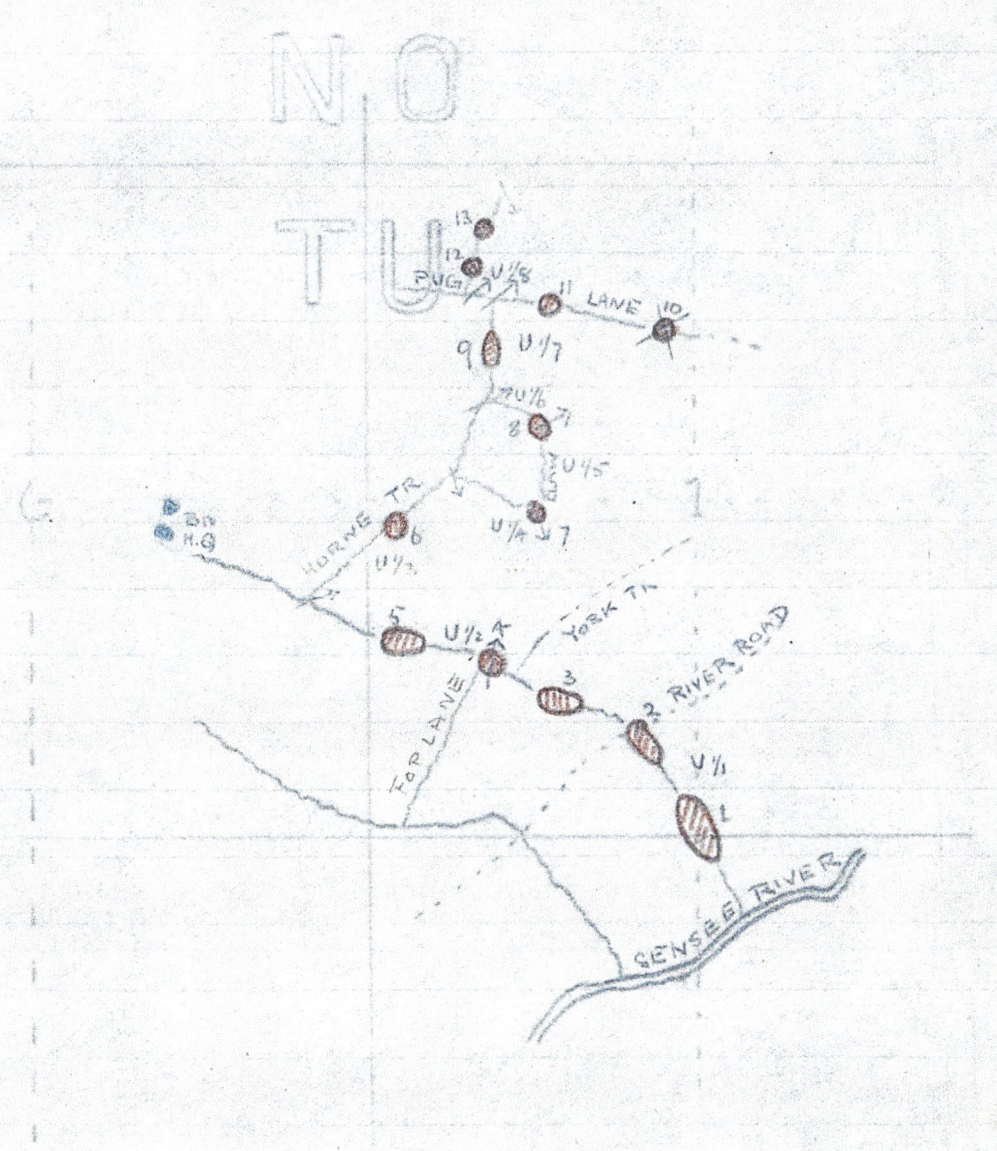

Operation Order No 3 by
O.C. "OXEN"

SECRET.
Copy No. 7

Ref Map
51 B.N.W.
Sketch att'd
August 21/8/17.

No.1. MOVE. The Battalion will relieve 12/13th Northumberland Fusiliers in the left Sector of the Brigade front on August 22nd. Companies will relieve correspondingly lettered Companies of the 12/13th Northumberland Fusiliers as follows:-
"A" Company on Right   Posts 1.2.& 3.
"B"   "   in Centre   "   4.5.6 & 7.
"C"   "   on Left   "   8.9 & 11.
"D"   "   in Support in "HIND TRENCH".

No.2. ROUTE and TIME. All Companies will proceed by Track running N.E. from Sunken Road at Pt T.10.a.0.0. in rear of Line of "C" Posts- then following the line of White Topped Pickets to the "RED FLAG".
Guides from 12/13th N.F. will meet Platoons there at 12-30 p.m. (Leading Company)

Companies will make their own way to Pt T.10.a.0.0. the leading Platoon of each Company to pass the Point as follows:-
"A" Company .... 12 noon.
"B"   "   .... 12.20 p.m.
"C"   "   .... 12.40 p.m.
"D"   "   .... 1 p.m.
Battn Headquarters .... 1.20 p.m.

Company Headquarters will move with the leading Platoons- there will always be five minutes interval between Platoons, distances must be maintained and there must be no closing up at T.10.a.0.0. or entrance to Communication Trench.

No.3. RATIONS. Dinners will be served about 7 p.m.- The food of the Tea Ration will be carried on man. Officers will make their own arrangements.

No.4. DRESS. Field Service Order.

No.5. ADVANCE PARTY. An advance party (as Detailed) will proceed to the Line at 10 a.m.

No.6. TRANSPORT. Special instructions are being issued.

No.7. RELIEF. All Trench stores, Defence schemes, Orders for working parties etc., will be taken over before relief by Officers attached in the Line. O.C.Companies will advise quantities taken over to Battalion Headquarters as soon as possible. Completion of Relief will be reported to Headquarters by code word "CARUSO".

V.F. Samuelson

Captain & Adjut.

COPY No 1. Filed
"   .. 2/5 O.C.Coy's
"   .. 6. T.O. & Q.M.
"   .. 7/8 War Diary.
"   .. 9   12/13th N.F.
"   ..10. R.S.M.
"   ..11/12 Filed.

SECRET VI

"OXEN" Provisional Defence Scheme   23.8.17

1. **Sector & Dispositions**   The Battalion holds the left sub-sector from PUG LANE to RIVER SENSEE (both inclusive.)
The Companies are disposed as follows—

"A" Right Coy (Head Quarters Tunnel U1c91)
   Front line — SHAFT TR POSTS 1–3
   Local support — 1 Platoon in Tunnel U1c91

"D" Centre Coy (H.Q. Tunnel T6d96)
   Front line — SHAFT TR Posts 4–5. HORN TR
   Post 6. junc. HORN and CLAW TR Post 7.
   Local Support 1 Platoon in Tunnel T6d96
      (1 M.G. between Posts 4 & 5

"C" Left Coy (H.Q. U1a2.6)
   Front line CLAW TR POSTS 8–9
      PUG LANE Post 11
   Local Support 1 Platoon U1a26

"B" Support Coy — ~~Platoon~~ in HIND and FIT TRENCHES

Each Coy will have 3 Lewis Guns in the front line and one with Coy Support Platoon.

The 50th DIVN is on our left — and the 1st BN LINCOLN REGT on our right.

Support: 1 Coy Support Bn in SHAFT TR (T6d)
and 1 Coy   "   "   . Posts C6 – C10 are at the disposal of O.C. 1/4th Queens.

II. **Action in case of Enemy Attack**

The line of Resistance is Front line posts, this must be held at all costs.

1. On attack threatening O.C. Coy whose area is threatened will immediately—
   (a) Stand to the whole of Company
   (b) Hold local support ready for immediate counter attack
   (c) Inform Coys on flanks & Battn. H.Q.

(2)

2. Battalion H.Q. will inform –
   (a) All units in Tunnel
   (b) Support Coys.

   All will stand to.

3. Should enemy gain a footing in our Trenches at any point.
   a) An immediate counter attack will be made by Coy concerned with the local supports – Bn H.Q. will be informed.
   (b) If this fails to dislodge him – the Support Coy will be used
   (c) Support Battalion Coys will only be used if Battalion Commander considers his own Support Company inadequate. Normally Advanced Posts in PUG LANE and CLAW TRENCH will be counter attacked from PUG LANE, therefore Support Coy should move by FIT and SHAFT and assemble in PUG LANE.

   Posts in SHAFT TRENCH will be normally counter attacked from HIND TR.

   In the event of a general attack developing the Coy of Support Battⁿ in SHAFT will be used for counter attack in PUG LANE – CLAW TR area, and Support Coy of this Battalion for SHAFT TR area.

   The Coy of Support Bn in "C" Posts 6-10 will be kept in hand as long as possible. In the event of Coy in SHAFT TR moving forward they will be ordered up to HIND TRENCH to replace it.

III. <u>Reconnaissance</u>. Officers and Senior N.C.Os. in Front line and Support Coys must thoroughly reconnoitre the ground and means of approach by day + night to facilitate quick movement.

IV. <u>Liaison</u>. All Support Coys will at once send an Officer to 'OXEN' H.Q. (Shaft 42) SHAFT on alarm.

V. <u>Communication</u> between Coys of Support Battalion in SHAFT and "C" Posts is established by Telephone.

VI. TACTICS. In the event of enemy entry he must be isolated by Trench Blocks and Gates. Bombing parties will hold flanks & enfilade fire will be brought to bear by L.G⁵ & Rifle Bombers.

O.C. Right Coy will be prepared to form a defensive flank in case of attack along SENSEE RIVER.

Support Coy of this Battⁿ would then be used to support this movement.

VII. Artillery. A Liaison Officer of 95th Bgde - covering our front - is at Bn. H.Q.

VIII. SIGNALS. The S.O.S. Signal is now 2 greens and 2 whites fired by Rifle.

"Lengthen Range" in case of Artillery firing in response to S.O.S. will be a series of Reds from a Very Pistol.

Flares will be lit if called for by Contact Aeroplane.

IX. Divˡ Trench Standing Orders & III Army Gas Standing Orders are to be followed.

(S) V. F. S.
Captain & Adjutant
Oxen

To All O.C. Coys
O.C. Support Coys

REPORT ON ACTION OF PATROL ON NIGHT OF 25/26.8.17.

    A Patrol of 1 Officer and 6 O/Rs. left No. 11 Post at about 11 p.m. for the purpose of verifying reports of Machine Gun Emplacements at approx. U.1.v.5.4. (Ref.51B)

    The Patrol proceeded to point U.1.b.4.3 having cut several lines of enemy wire, and there lay under cover observing machine gun fire and enemy parties working on the parapets of trenches about 15 yards East of it.

    After a time 2/Lt. H.S.Gilliland and No.202449 Lce/Sgt W.N. Goatcher started to get forward under enemy wire. Owing to the thickness of the wire and to its being practically on the enemy parapet it was not possible to use wire cutters, but after a considerable time both managed to get under the wire and on to the enemy parapet unseen. They found the trenches very deep, 9' to 12', and sentry posts at short intervals; a carrying party was passing down trench in an S. direction with Trench Mortar shells. The trench was found to run parallel to Rotten Row and the M.G.Emplacements were on the West side of trenches. Four M.Gs. were observed to fire from mound immediately East of road. After waiting about three quarters of an hour on the parapet 2/Lt. H.S.Gilliland and No.202449 L/S W.N.Goatcher rejoined the patrol, and decided that owing to the number of enemy in the trench and the various obstacles which had to be encountered it was impossible to obtain identification. It was therefore decided to withdraw. Almost immediately heavy M.G.fire was opened on the party. 2/Lt. Gilliland was wounded in the arm, and No. 206110 Pte H.Homewood was wounded in a similar manner; No.205372 L/Cpl H.P.Matthews was seen to fall, and was found to be severely wounded in the abdomen. He refused all help and asked to be left so that the Patrol could withdraw from the heavy fire. No.205372 L/C Matthews then managed to crawl on for some 200 yards, when, being exhausted, No.206110 Pte H.Homewood and 2/Lt. H.S.Gilliland in turn carried him on their backs for the remainder of the distance.

    Machine Gun fire did not stop until the patrol reached our trenches about 3.5 a.m. The withdrawl was covered by No.201669 L/Sgt H.Blakeman, No.202418 Pte J.Rosenbaum, and No.205503 Pte W.G.Painter.

    2/Lt. H.S.Gilliland states that he cannot speak too highly of the conduct of the whole Patrol, three being particularly noticeable in their conduct, viz:-
        No.202449 L/Sgt W.N.Goatcher
        " 205372 L/Cpl H.P.Matthews,
        " 206110 Pte. H.Homewood,
all of whom showed the greatest courage.

                                                        Lieut.Col.
            Commanding 3/4th Bn. "The Queen's" (RWS) Regt.

SECRET.   OPERATION ORDER No. 4.   Copy No. 11

Ref. Sheet 51 B. S.W.   August 26th, 1917.

1. **RELIEF.** The Battalion will be relieved in the Front Line by 8th Royal Dublin Fusiliers tomorrow the 27th inst. and will move to Huts, HAMELINCOURT (A.5.a.7.8.) Companies will be relieved by correspondingly lettered Company.

2. **ROUTE.** "A" & "D" Companies will use FIT LANE, "C" PUG LANE and FIT LANE, "B" HIND TRENCH, thence by overland route to BOYELLES and HAMELINCOURT.

3. **GUIDES.** Two guides per Company and 1 for Battn. H.Qs. will rendezvous at POST C.10 at 11.30 a.m. and proceed to 62nd Bde. H.Qs., reporting 1 p.m. to conduct respective Companies of incoming Unit to Front Line Companies.
O.C. Scouts will detail 1 guide to report 62nd Inf. Bde. H.Qs. at 10 a.m. to bring Advance Party of incoming Unit to Battn. Hd.Qs. except the Sergeant Cook, who will be left at STALEY BRIDGE.

4. **LEWIS GUNS.** All Lewis Guns will be dumped at POST C.10, on relief each Company detailing a Guard of 1 N.C.O. and 2 men to remain until arrival of two Limbers, one for "A" & "B" Coys., one for "C" & "D" Companies.

5. **HANDING OVER.** All Trench Stores, Defence Schemes, Maps (except Trench Canvas Maps) and Aeroplane Photographs will be handed over, lists of above to be sent to Battn. H.Q. by 8 p.m.

6. **RELIEF COMPLETE** "Relief Complete" will be wired to Batt. H.Q. by Code Word "YELNATS" and Companies will move independently to HAMELINCOURT at once, intervals of 5 minutes between Platoons. Batt. H.Q. will move on orders from Adjutant. The distances will be corrected before leaving the Trench at RED FLAG.

7. **DISCIPLINE.** All Shelters, Cookhouses and Company H.Qrs. to be left scrupulously clean. Strict march discipline will be maintained.

8. **ADMINISTRATIVE ORDERS.** Follow.

9. **ADVANCE PARTIES.** The Advance Party of incoming Unit will consist of 1 Officer & 1 N.C.O. per Company, Regtl. Sergt. Major, Sergt. Cook, 2 Signallers per Company, 3 Signallers Battn. H.Qrs.

10. **OFFICERS' KITS.** 1 G.S. Wagon will leave Point C.10 at 3 p.m. to convey Officers' Kits, Company Canteens, etc. to HAMELINCOURT. (See Administrative Orders.)

Issued by Runners.

Copy No. 1   File.
"   " 2/5 Company Commanders.
"   "   6   Q.M. & T.O.
"   "   7   Commanding Officer.
"   "   8   62nd Infantry Brigade.
"   "   9   R.S.M.
"   " 10   Batt. H.Qrs. & Lieut. Carter.
"   " 11/12 War Diary.

In the Field.
26.8.17.
                                                            Captain,
                                                      Adjutant, OXEN.

SECRET.   OPERATION ORDER No. 5.   Copy No. 8.

Ref. Sheet 11, LENS.   27.8.17.

1. **MOVE.** The Battalion will move into Billets at WARLUS tomorrow.

2. **ROUTE & TIME.** The Route will be as follows:- BOIRY ST. MARTIN - FICHEUX - WAILY - WARLUS, distance about 10 miles. 100 yards will be maintained between Companies on the march.
   Headquarters will leave Camp at 10.15 a.m. followed at 100 yards interval by Companies in alphabetical order.

3. **DISCIPLINE.** The strictest march discipline will be maintained. The Huts will be left thoroughly cleaned.

4. **TRANSPORT.** The Transport will accompany the Battalion - special instructions are being issued. All L.G.Wagons will be loaded by 9 a.m. under Company arrangements.

5. **DRESS.** Battle Order. Waterproof sheets outside haversack. Packs will be conveyed by lorry and will be marked and stacked by Companies at Q.M.Stores by 9 a.m.

6. **RATIONS.** A haversack ration will be issued for midday - Dinners will be served after arrival, and teas at 7.30 p.m.

7. **OFFICERS' KITS.** will be ready for loading by 9 a.m. at Q.M.Stores.

8. **SICK** and men unable to march will parade at Orderly Room at 9.15 a.m.

9. **DRUMS.** The Drums will parade as a separate section.

10. **ADVANCE PARTY.** Will proceed to Warlus by Lorry, reporting at Orderly Room at 9.15 a.m.

11. **REPORTS** to head of "A" Company.

Issued by Orderly at 10.15 p.m.

Copy No. 1/4 Company Commanders.
 "   "   5 Q.M.
 "   "   6 T.O.
 "   "   7 Filed.
 "   "   8/9 War Diary.

                                        Captain,
                              Adjutant,   OXEN.

3/4th Bn. "THE QUEEN'S" (R.W.S) REGIMENT.

Nominal Roll of Officers.

Substantive Rank.	Acting Rank.	Name.	
Major	A/Lieut.Col.	K.A.Oswald.	
Captain	A/Major	A.H.Harper.	
Lieutenant		T.S.Smith.	
"	A/Captain	A.T.Latham.	
"	A/Captain	P.M.Hepworth.	
"	A/Captain & Adjutant	V.F.Samuelson.	
"		E.W.Preston.	
"	A/Captain	L.J.C.Vidler.	
"	A/Captain	C.G.Moss.	
"	A/Captain	G.A.Ionides.	
" & Q.M.		T.I.Birch.	
"		J.J.Brooke	2/6 Suffolk Regt. (attached).
2/Lieut.	A/Captain	H.P.McCabe	
"	A/Lieut.	H.W.Carter.	
"	A/Lieut.	A.B.Frost.	
"	A/Lieut.	F.W.A.Buckell.	
"	A/Lieut.	R.R.B.Bannerman.	
"	A/Lieut.	G.A.Shaw.	
"	A/Lieut.	A.H.A.Cooper.	
"		J. Ost.	10th Devons. (attached).
"		P.A.Curtois	2/6 Suffolk Regt. (attached).
"		A.H.Lovell.	
"		E.H.Dakin.	
"		D.R.J.O'Connor.	
"		A.H.John.	
"		H.E.Fisk.	
"		W.P.Thomas.	1st London. (attached).
"		S.J.Mason.	2/6 Suffolk Reft. (attached).
"		A.E.Barrow.	
"		J.R.Skeet.	2nd London (attached).
"		H.S.Gilliland.	1st Devons (attached).
"		G.P.Cockburn.	2/6 Suffolk Regt. (attached).
"		N.H.Sisterson.	12th Northumberland Fus.(attached).
"		J.C.Davie.	5th Royal Fus. (attached).
"		C.A.Freestone.	do. do.
"		S.Hall.	13th Northumberland Fus.(attached).
"		C.Seyler.	13th London Regt. (attached).
"		J.H.Shepperd.	
"		W.Wallace.	
"		B.A.Shortman.	

Captain A.E.Mackenzie, R.A.M.C. (T) (attached).

Rev. M. Tron, C.E., C.F. (attached).

Lieut.Colonel,
Commanding 3/4th Bn."The Queen's" (RWS)Regt.

September 1st, 1917.

Army Form C. 2118

WAR DIARY
or
INTELLIGENCE SUMMARY
(Erase heading not required.)

3rd Queens R Regt

Place	Date 1917	Hour	Summary of Events and Information	Remarks and references to Appendices
WARLUS	Sept. 1.		Strength of Battalion 42 Officers 866 other ranks	M.C.C.
	3.		Training Continued. new methods of attack against latest enemy system of defence taught for the first time.	M.C.C.
do.	4.		Training Continued. 202549 2/Sgt. GOATCHER. W.N. awarded Military Medal for work performed during the night 25/26 August 1917. (vid Appendix VII A.F.C.2118 for Aug. not).	Appendix I M.C.C.
do.	5.		Training Continued	M.C.C.
do.	6.		Training Continued	M.C.C.
do.	7.		Training Continued	M.C.C.
do.	8.		Training Continued	M.C.C.
do.	10.		Training Continued	M.C.C.
do.	11.		Training Continued. Captain H.C. CANNON. M.C. 1st Batt. "The Queens" took over duties of 2nd in Command	M.C.C.
do.	12.		Training Continued. 2nd/Lieut. H.S. GILLILAND. awarded Military Cross for work performed during the night 25/26 August 1917 (vid Appendix VIII A.F.C.2118 for Aug not).	Appendix II M.C.C.
do.	13.		Training Continued	M.C.C.
do.	14.		Training Continued	M.C.C.
do.	15.		Training Continued	M.C.C.

1875. Wt. W593/826 1,000,000 4/15 J.B.C. & A. A.P.S.S./Forms/C. 2118.

WAR DIARY or INTELLIGENCE SUMMARY

Army Form C. 2118

Place	Date	Hour	Summary of Events and Information	Remarks and references to Appendices
WARLUS	September 1917 16		Move to CAESTRE in area of X Corps, II Army. Marched from WARLUS, 5.15 p.m. & entrained at SAVY 10.45 p.m.	Appendix III M.C.C
CAESTRE	17		Detrained 9.30 a.m. & billeted in farms around hamlet of LE PEUPLIER, S.W. of CAESTRE. 'C' Coy. arrived 2.0 p.m. Brigade H.Q. situated at BORRÉ.	M.C.C
do.	18		Training continued. Draft of 100 O.R. of 9/ "The Buffs" arrived from the Base.	M.C.C
do.	19		Training continued. Draft of 60 O.R. arrived from the Base. Meeting with 8th. Batt. also "The Queen's" Regiment commanded by Lt. Col. Trenchen D.S.O. they were situated around ROUGE CROIX.	M.C.C
do.	20		Training continued.	M.C.C
do.	21		Training continued.	M.C.C
do.	22		Training continued. 2nd Lieut. R.B. Sparkes 9/5 Battalion "The Queen's" Regiment was attached for duty.	M.C.C
do.	23		Move to LE ROUKLOSHILLE Area. Marched from LE PEUPLIER at 9.0 a.m. via ROUGE CROIX & FLETRE arriving in billeting area about 10.30 a.m. The battalion was billeted in farms S. & S.E. of MONT des CATS. Brigade Hd. situated at LE ROUKLOSHILLE. General Sir Herbert Plumer G.O.C. 2nd Army visited the battalion whilst at training & expressed satisfaction with all he saw. Meeting with nucleus party of 1st Battalion "The Queen's" Regiment situated at PIEBROUCK W. of BERTHEN.	Appendix IV M.C.C
LE ROUKLOSHILLE	24			M.C.C
do.	25		Training continued.	M.C.C
do.	26		Training continued.	M.C.C
do.	27		Training continued.	M.C.C

Army Form C. 2118

WAR DIARY
or
INTELLIGENCE SUMMARY
(Erase heading not required.)

Place	Date	Hour	Summary of Events and Information	Remarks and references to Appendices
LE ROUKLOSHILLE	September 28		Move to MERSEN. The Battalion marched from LE ROUKLOSHILLE Area at 11:40 a.m. via BERTHEN + BOESINGHE arriving at KENORA Camp, S.W. of RENING HELST, at 1:5 p.m. The Battalion was accommodated in Huts, huts & bivouacs.	Appendix Y. ICC
RENINGHELST	29		Training Continued. Hostile aircraft active in neighbourhood of Camp throughout the earlier part of the night.	ICC
do	30		Move to ZILLEBEKE. The Battalion, less Nucleus Party of 9 officers + 100 O.R. left KENORA Camp at 2:30 p.m. & marched via WESTOUTRE, LA CLYTTE + VOORMEZEELE The Battalion was situated in trenches + shelters on northern bank of the ÉTANG de ZILLEBEKE. The Transport + Quartermaster's Stores were situated at SCOTTISH WOOD, East of ÉTANG de DICKEBUSCH. The Nucleus Party remained at KENORA CAMP under command of Major Harper. 2nd Lieut. T. CALVERT was posted for duty.	Appendix Y. ICC

K.O.Oswald
Lieut. Colonel.
Commanding 3/4 Battalion
"The Queen's" Regiment.

Appendix. I

Extract from :-

21st. DIVISION
ROUTINE ORDERS.

Saturday, 8th September 1917.

957. HONOURS & REWARD.

The General Officer Commanding has much pleasure in announcing the following award :-

The MILITARY MEDAL.

No. 202449 Corporal (L/Sgt) W. N. Goatcher,
The (Queen's) Royal West Surrey Regt.

Sergeant Goatcher was sent on a patrol to report on enemy Machine Gun positions. He crawled through the wire and lay on the enemy parapet for three-quarters of an hour.
As the patrol was withdrawing, heavy fire was opened, and an Officer and two men of the patrol were wounded. Sergeant Goatcher helped to bring them back. He showed great coolness and bravery, and his report on the enemy's trenches and disposition of his Machine Guns was of great value.

Appendix II

Extract from:-

CORPS ROUTINE ORDERS
BY
Lieutenant-General J.A.L. Haldane, C.B., D.S.O.,
Commanding VI Corps.

11th September, 1917.

ADJUTANT-GENERAL'S BRANCH.

2650. HONOURS & REWARDS.
The Army & Corps Commanders have been pleased to note that the Field Marshal Commanding-in-Chief has, under authority granted by His Majesty the King, awarded the Military Cross to the undermentioned officer. The recipient should be informed, if possible. His name will be published in the London Gazette in due course.

21st Division.
2/Lieut. H. S. Gilliland, Devon Regt, attd. E.S. Surrey Regt.

SECRET.   COPY No. 11.

Appendix III

OPERATION ORDER No.6 BY
Lieut Colonel K.A.Oswald Commanding OXEN.

Ref:- Map - Lens, Sheet 11 &   15.9.17.
51c.

1. The Division will move by train from this Area to the Second Army Area on September 16th and 17th.

2. The Battalion, less "C" Company and one Cooker, will move by road as under on the 16th inst., to SAVY and entrain for CAESTRE (Train No.17). Rendezvous Cross roads in WARLUS, K36.d.5.7. at 6.15 p.m. "A" Company facing South- "B" Company in rear of "A" Company- "D" Company facing West- Battalion H.Qrs facing North- Acting Drummers, as a separate section, facing East.

3. Special instructions re Transport Section and "C" Company's hour of move are issued with Administrative instruction No.1.

4. Loading party at the Station will be provided by the 12/13th Northumberland Fusiliers.

5. All ranks must be warned that they are not to climb on the roofs of trucks or sit with their legs outside the trucks.
   The trains will be type Omnibus i.e. One Coach, 30 covers, 17 flats.

6. Rations for the 17th inst will be carried under Q.M's arrangements in bulk.

7. Railhead, from 16th September inclusive, will be CAESTRE.

8. All billets and huts must be left thoroughly clean and a certificate sent to Battalion Headquarters by 5.p.m. 16th inst. by all O.C. Companies and Battalion Headquarters Company that this has been done.
   Tents will be handed over to the Town Major by 3.p.m. and receipts taken.

9. Route to place of entrainment WARLUS- AGNEZ-lez- DUISANS- HAUTES- AVESNES- hence by main road to SAVY.

10. Dress:- Field service order.

11. Reports to head of "A" Company after leaving WARLUS.

[signature]
Captain & Adjutant,
"OXEN"

Issued by Runner at   on 15.9.17.

Copy No. 1 Filed.
"   "   2-6 Coy Commanders & H.Q.Coy.
"   "   7 62nd Inf.Brigade H.Qrs.
"   "   8 Quartermaster.
"   "   9 Transport Officer.
"   "   10 R.S.M.
"   "   11 War Diary.
"   "   12 ditto.

ADMINISTRATION INSTRUCTION No.1 for

MOVE to 2nd. ARMY AREA.

15.9.17.

1. The Transport Section, less "C" Coy Cooker, will leave WARLUS on the 16th inst., at 4.45 p.m., for SAVY.
Route to be taken same as Para 9: O.O. No.6.

2. The train(No.17) leaves SAVY for CAESTRE at 23.28, 16th inst, and the transport section will be there 3 hours before departure.

3. Horses will be entrained saddled up.

4. D.A.Q.M.G. 21st Div. will be in charge of entrainment to SAVY and Staff Captain under Orders of D.A.A.G. 21st Div. will be responsible for detrainment.

5. Arrangements re Sick will be issued later.

6. All mounted Officers, except O.C. "C" Coy, will ride their Horses to SAVY, and their grooms must accompany them in order that the Horses can be entrained immediately on arrival.

7. Each man will carry a Haversack Ration for the night, and teas will be served by 3.30.p.m. where Cookers or Dixies are used. (O.C. "C" Coy., will make his own arrangements).
Breakfasts will be served from Company Cookers on arrival at new destination.

8. All Officers' Valises must be deposited at Q.M.Stores by 2.30.p.m 16th inst.
Coy. Lewis Gun Limbers and Cookers must be loaded under Coy arrangements by 2.30.p.m., 16th inst.

9. "C" Company and one Cooker will leave WARLUS at 12 midnight by Route March, same route as Battalion, reporting to Entraining Officer at 4.a.m. at SAVY Station and proceed by train No.21 at 5.28.a.m., on the 17th inst.

10. Guides will be at CAESTRE Station to meet both trains.

11. Lieutenant A.H.A.Cooper is detailed to receive and attend to any claims for damage which cannot be dealt with by the Commanding Officer before departure. (G.R.O. 1146).

Captain & Adjutant,
"OXEN"

Appendix IX

OPERATION ORDER No.7.
by
Lieut Colonel K.A.Oswald,

Commanding "OXEN".

SECRET.

COPY No. 11

MAP REF:- Sheet 27.   22.9.17.

1. The 62nd Infantry Brigade will move tomorrow 23rd inst to LE ROUKLOSHILLE area by route march.

2. The Battalion will parade ready to move off as under:-

   Headquarters Coy,   - Head of Coy,   W.7.a.9.9.   Facing WEST.
   "A" Company,   -   do   W.7.a.6.9.   do   EAST.
   "B" Company,   -   do   W.7.a.6.7.   Road Junction.
   "C" Company,   - Outside Coy H.Qrs.   Facing EAST.
   "D" Company,   - Head of Coy,   W.7.b.2.6.   Road Junction.
   Transport in rear of "D" Company.
   AT 9.a.m.

3. The following distances will be observed on line of march.
   Between Companies 100 yards,
   Between last Company and Transport 100 yards.

4. Further instructions will be issued re Billeting parties.

5. The strictest march discipline will be maintained on the march.

6. Officers valises will be at Q.M.stores and Company Officers Mess surplus at H.Qrs Mess by 8.a.m.
   O.C.Transport will detail one limber to report to "D"Coy,H.Qrs at 7.15 a.m. and proceed to "C" Company's H.Qrs by 7.30 a.m. to convey above.

7. O.C. "B" Company will detail a loading party of 1 N.C.O. and 10 men to report at Q.M.stores at 7.45 a.m.
   Same Company will detail 1 N.C.O. and 10 men to report at Transport lines at 8.a.m. to act as loaders and escorts.

8. Sick parade will be at 7.15 a.m. and any men marked unfit to march will report at M.O's sick room at 8.30.a.m. carrying Haversack ration.

9. O&C.Companies will render a certificate to this Office kaxthis by 8.30 a.m. stating all Billets are left thoroughly clean.

10. Reveille will be at 5 a.m.

11. Mid-day meal will be issued from Company Cookers, (Cooked en route) and Cookers will accompany respective Companies. Headquarters Company's rations will be carried under Q.M. arrangements, and served on arrival.
    O.C.Transport will send Horses to respective Companies' Headquarters for Cookers by 8.15 a.m.

                                                    Captain & Adjutant,
                                                          "OXEN"

issued by Orderly Sergts at 11 p.m.
         22.9.17.

Copy No. 1. Filed.
  "   "   2 to 6 Coys & H.Qrs Coy,
  "   "   7   Q.M.
  "   "   8   T.O.
  "   "   9   R.S.M.
  "   " 10   62nd Inf.Bde.Hqrs.
  "   " 11 & 12 War Diary.

OPERATION ORDER No. 8.
by Lieut.Col.K.A.Oswald
Commanding OXEN.

Copy No.

Map Ref. HAZEBROUCK 5a.   28.9.17.

1. The 62nd Inf. Brigade group will move by route march to-day 28th inst. to No. 7 area Sheet 28 M.2.

2. The Battalion will rendezvous at Cross Roads 3.I.1¾.3½ at 11.10 a.m.

3. The following distances will be observed between Companies and Transport Section - 100 yards.

4. The strictest march discipline will be maintained on the march.

5. Advance billeting parties of 1 N.C.O. per Company and Sgt.Ford for Bn.H.Q.Coy. mounted on bicycles will rendezvous at above (para.2) at 9.0 a.m. and report to Lieut. R.R.B.Bannerman and proceed to M.8.c.1.3 (sheet 28) and report to Staff Captain, 62nd Infantry Brigade by 10.0 a.m.

6. Administration orders issued herewith.

7. Acknowledge.

Captain & Adjutant.
OXEN.

Issued at 7.30 a.m. by runner.

Copy No. 1 Filed.
   2/6 Companies & H.Q.Coy.
    7 62nd Inf. Bde.
    8 M.O.
    9 T.O.
   10 Q.M.
   11/12 War Diary.

Appendix V

ADMINISTRATION ORDER NO. 1
in conjunction with O.O. No. 8.

1. O.C. "D" Coy. will detail a loading party to report Q.M. Stores at 8.30 a.m. and will rejoin Coy. in time to move with Coy.. O.C. "C" Co. will detail 1 N.C.O & 10 men to report T.Offr. at 9.30 a.m. to act as escort and loaders to pack animals.

2. Any men marked "Unfit" to march by the M.O. will report at Q.M. Stores with haversack ration by 12 noon. The sick at Batt. Headquarters now will be conveyed by motor lorry to new destination. Capt. A.T. Latham will be in charge of the party. Special instructions have been issued him. Haversack rations must be issued.

3. O.C. Coys. and H.Q. Coy. will render a certificate at rendezvous that all billets have been left thoroughly clean. O.C. Coys. will render an occupation return to the Quartermaster before 10.0 a.m.

4. Midday meal will be cooked en route and served on arrival. Cookers and Lewis Gun limbers will accompany Companies en route. O.C. Transport will send horses to be at respective Companies as under:-

    "A" Coy. 10. 0 a.m.
    "B" "   10.45 a.m.
    "C" "   10. 0 a.m.
    "D" "   10.30 a.m.

Headquarter Coy. will have midday meal served on arrival at new destination.

5. The Quartermaster will send at once 1 G.S. Waggon to collect Officers' kits of "A" and "B" Coys. - 1 G.S. Waggon to collect "C" Co. and Bn. Headquarters. Both will return to Q.M. Stores on completion of duty.

6. T.O. will send tool limbers to Q.M. Stores by 9.30 a.m., Bomb Limber to Bn.H.Q. by 9.0 a.m. to collect Signal stores.

Captain & Adjutant.
OXEN.

OPERATION ORDER No. 9.   Copy No. 10

by Lieut.Col.K.A.Oswald
Commanding O X E N.

Map.Ref. Sheet 28.   30.9.17.

1. The 62nd Infantry Bde. will send one Battalion to a position South of ZILLEBEKE to-day, 30th inst.

2. The Battalion will move to-day at 2.30 p.m. - following order:- "A" Co. - "B" Co. - "C" Co. - "D" Co. - Transport Section. 100 yards intervals will be kept between Platoons and Sections of Transport on the line of march.

3. Cookers will accompany respective Companies, all remainder of Transport will be under the Transport Officer.

4. Cross Country Tracks will be used as far as possible.

5. The Battalion will be accommodated in I.21.d between Lake and the Railway.

6. Th Acknowledge.

(Sgd.) V.F.Samuelson,
Captain & Adjutant.
O X E N.

Issued by Orderly at 12 noon.

Copy No. 1   Filed.
 "   " 2/6   Companies & H.Q.Coy.
 "   "   7   62nd Inf. Brigade.
 "   "   8   T.O.
 "   "   9   Q.M.
 "   " 10/11 War Diary.

SUBJECT.

6²/₁

No.	Contents.	Date.
	3/4 Queens RW Surrey's October 1917	

Appendix 3

MAP SHOWING "DISPOSITIONS BEFORE AND AFTER ATTACK ON OCTOBER 4TH 1917.
POLYGONE de ZONNEBEKE
Jetty Wood
Jetty
Trench
Jubilee Croft
Jolting Houses
JOLTING TRENCH
JUNIPER TRENCH
Jetty Warren
Reutel
Ce.my
Judge Copse
Judge Cott.
Judge Cross Roads
Zwaanhoek
Cemy
Joist Fm
Polygonebeek
D Coy
A Coy
Bn. H.Q.
2nd Objective
Positions Prior to Attack
After the withdrawal from 1st objective
Approx. Consolidation of Battalion at 1st objective
Scale 1: 5,000
Yards
250
500
850 Yards
1/4
1/2 Mile

WAR DIARY
or
INTELLIGENCE SUMMARY

Army Form C. 2118

Place	Date	Hour	Summary of Events and Information	Remarks and references to Appendices
ZILLEBEKE	OCTOBER		Strength of Battalion. 44 Officers 938 other ranks	
do.	2		The day was spent in drawing stores preparatory to taking over in the front line. The enemy artillery was active in the vicinity. Casualties. 1 O.R. killed. The Battalion relieved the 9th Leicestershire Regiment, 110th Brigade on front line. Dispositions 'A' Company on the right, 'D' Company on the left, on the front line, 'B' Company in support, 'C' Company in reserve. The Battalion area shelled with shrapnel and H.E. whilst moving up. Apart to take cover. Sunset Night. Casualties. 1 Officer & O.R. wounded	N.E.C. Appendix 1. Appendix 2.
Frezen S.E. of POLYGON WOOD	3		A quiet day with intermittent shell fire. Final operation orders were issued as to the attack. Casualties. 2 officers wounded 2d. 1 O.R. killed 10 O.R. wounded.	Appendix 2.
do.	4		At 4.30 a.m. the Battalion completed the dispositions for the attack, 'B' Company moving up between 'A' & 'D' Companies who had 'C' Company moved up in close support; the manoeuvre was carried out quickly & without difficulty. At Zero, 6.00 a.m. the Battalion advanced to the assault, the 16th Royal Warwickshire being on the right & the 1st Bedfordshire Regiment, 7th Division on its left. A certain amount of difficulty was experienced crossing the POLYGON BEEK, after which the hostile defences were encountered, only slight opposition was offered to the advance which proceeded quickly except in the centre of 'B' Company where a concrete fortine put up a strong resistance which was soon overcome. The objective was reached up to time & rapidly consolidated. At Zero + 130 minutes the barrage advanced towards the 2nd objective the 1st Lincolnshire Regt on the left & 1st 12/13 Northumberland Fusiliers on the right advanced, captured &	Appendix 3 do. 7 do. 8 do. 9 do. 10

WAR DIARY or INTELLIGENCE SUMMARY

Army Form C. 2118

(Erase heading not required.)

Place	Date	Hour	Summary of Events and Information	Remarks and references to Appendices
Trenches S.E. of POLYGON WOOD	OCTOBER 4th.		Consolidated the 2nd objective. Two Companies of the troops who had captured the 2nd objective returned to hold the 1st. objective, leaving the Battalion forthwith on JETTY WARREN where they again dug themselves in, "A" & "B" Companies in front with "C" & "D" Companies in close support. The enemy artillery maintained a continuous barrage over the whole area captured, casualties few however. Great difficulty was experienced in clearing the wounded. At 7.0.P. in the enemy made a counter attack on the right which was however dispersed by our artillery fire. The enemy shelled the back area throughout the night. Their counter but communication & removal of wounded was extremely difficult. Casualties, Officers 3 killed 6 wounded. O.R. 49 killed 184 wounded 19 missing	H.E.C.
do.	5.		Hostile artillery extremely active at dawn. Lt. Col. R. A. OSWARD was wounded whilst reconnoitring the front positions. Captain L. J. SAMUELSON took command of the Battalion. The day was spent in improving the positions of the Battalion, enemy shell fire at all times heavy, especially during the night. S.O.S. signals were sent up twice on the right flank of Brigade front but no hostile infantry attack eventuated. Upon the Battn 6.2nd Brigade Time. Casualties: Officers 1 wounded. O.R. 1 killed 20 wounded 1 missing.	Appendices. 5. " 7 " 8 H.E.C.
do.	6.		Enemy gun fire again very active throughout the day. The 10th Yorkshire Regiment which had been in close support to the Battalion, relieved the 1st Lancashire Regt. on 12/13 Northumberland Fusiliers in front line. The dispositions of the Battalion remained as before. Hostile artillery active throughout the night. Casualties. Officers 1 wounded. O.R. 2 killed 5 wounded.	Appendices. 3.

Army Form C. 2118

WAR DIARY
or
INTELLIGENCE SUMMARY
(Erase heading not required.)

Place	Date	Hour	Summary of Events and Information	Remarks and references to Appendices
Trenches East of POLYGON WOOD	OCTOBER 7.		Hostile artillery slightly quieter throughout the day. Officers of 1st Battalion Royal Welsh Fusiliers reconnoitred the line. The Battalion was relieved by 1 Company 1st Royal Welsh Fusiliers, 7th Division, relief being complete by 3.0 a.m October 8. Casualties O.R. 3 killed 9 wounded.	M.C.C. Appendix 4.
do.	8.		Very quiet night, relief proceeded quietly & without any difficulty. The Battalion was accommodated in Dubbies &c in &nearby Southern bank of ZILLEBEKE LAKE. Appalling weather conditions during the night, many of the men suffered from lack of shelter. Casualties Officers 1 wounded.	M.C.C
ZILLEBEKE	9.		At 10.45 a.m. An order was received to proceed to SCOTTISH WOOD which destination was reached about 12 noon. The men were given the remainder of the day to rest (their equipment). The equipment was covered at 1.30 p.m. The DICKEBUSCH ROAD from which entrained at 3.15 p.m. The Battalion were entrained at 5.0 p.m. the remainder to ERQUINGHEM arriving at 10.30 p.m. Thence the Battalion marched to SERCUS where the companies were billeted in farms on the outskirts of the village.	M.C.C Appendix 11.
SERCUS	10.		Day devoted to rest & cleaning up. Casualties O.R. 4 killed 3 wounded.	M.C.C.
do.	11.		Training Commenced.	M.C.C Appendix. 6
do.	12.		Training Continued.	M.C.C.
do.	13.		Training Continued. The Battalion was congratulated by G.O.C. 21st Division.	M.C.C.

WAR DIARY
or
INTELLIGENCE SUMMARY
(Erase heading not required.)

Army Form C. 2118

Instructions regarding War Diaries and Intelligence Summaries are contained in F.S. Regs., Part II. and the Staff Manual respectively. Title Pages will be prepared in manuscript.

Place	Date	Hour	Summary of Events and Information	Remarks and references to Appendices
AERCUS	OCTOBER 15		Training Continued	M.C.C
do.	16		Training Continued	M.C.C
do.	17		Training Continued	M.C.C
do.	18		Training Continued	M.C.C
do.	19		Training Continued. 7 N.C.Os from the Battalion were awarded the D.C.M. Division & Corps Officers for work done during operations from Oct 2 to Oct 7.	M.C.C
do.	20		Move to DICKEBUSCH Area. The Battalion, less leaving SERCUS at 3:45 p.m. marched to EBLINGHEM Station, entraining at 9.30 p.m. and arriving at DICKEBUSCH Station at 2.45 a.m. thence marching to MICMAC CAMP. The Battalion being all in by 4.30 a.m. The transport had left SERCUS on the day at 11.30 p.m. making for the night in the GRAVES area.	Appendix 12. M.C.C Appendix 13.
MICMAC CAMP. W. of DICKEBUSCH	21.		The Transport arrived at about 12 noon. At 3.45 p.m. the Battalion moved to Camp near KRUISSTRAATHOEK, comprising Officers and 4 Officers 19 O.R. left to reconnoitre the line. Portable cookhouses arrived at vicinity of Camp during the night. The commanding Officer left to reconnoitre the lines at 5.0 p.m.	M.C.C
CAMP near KRUISSTRAATHOEK	22.		At 10.30 p.m. to ZILLEBEKE LAKE where dinners were served. Hence to HOOGE CRATER (Brigade Head Quarters) where Guides of the 10th West Yorkshire Regiment, 69th Brigade, 23rd Division were met. The battalion being led by platoons, "A" Company, "B" Company on the Left, in the front line. "A" Company was on the night. "C" Company was in immediate Support & comp⟨any⟩ attacking Coy forming ⟨the⟩ relief. "D" Company was in reserve. The night it was fine & ⟨was?⟩ heavy artillery firing quiet, the relief being completed at 12 midnight. Casualties O.R. 2 killed & 4 wounded.	M.C.C Appendix 14, 15

WAR DIARY or INTELLIGENCE SUMMARY

Army Form C. 2118.

(Erase heading not required.)

Instructions regarding War Diaries and Intelligence Summaries are contained in F.S. Regs., Part II and the Staff Manual respectively. Title pages will be prepared in manuscript.

Hour, Date, Place	Summary of Events and Information	Remarks and references to Appendices
Trenches on REUTEL RIDGE East of POLYGON WOOD. OCTOBER 23	Heavy hostile shelling from about 3.30 a.m. until daylight searching all ground from just behind front line to Eastern edge of POLYGON WOOD. The 29th Battalion Australian Infantry on our immediate left & 10th Yorkshire Regiment on our right, we are in touch with both units. Enemy artillery active throughout the day. Quiet this evening. A Company sent a patrol up JOINER'S AVENUE & found an enemy machine gun & a few men about 200 East o/A Company HQ. "C" Company patrolled to their left front, finding no trace of the enemy & an occupied concrete dug out. Casualties. O.R. 2 killed 4 wounded. Quiet night.	H.C.C. Appendix. 15
do. 24	Enemy artillery again extremely active about dawn & throughout most of day putting up a strong retaliation to our practice barrages, his barrage lines being along BECELAERE road just West of front line, also a line due North / South through Battalion H.Q. An Inter. Company Relief was successfully carried out during the Latter part of the evening, the hostile guns being quiet for the most part. "B" Company relieved A Company & "D" Company relieved "C" Coy, who went into immediate support, A Company going into reserve.	H.C.C. Appendix 16 " 17

WAR DIARY or INTELLIGENCE SUMMARY.

(Erase heading not required.)

Army Form C. 2118.

Hour, Date, Place	Summary of Events and Information	Remarks and references to Appendices
Trenches RECTEN RIDGE EAST of POLYGON WOOD. OCTOBER. 5th and 2nd	The relief being completed by 9.30 p.m. "B" Company sent out a patrol to reconnoitre at T.6.a.8.0. No traces of the enemy were found. Casualties: O.R. 3 killed, 9 wounded.	
do. 23.	Enemy artillery question though troublesome shelling of whole Battalion area throughout the day. MAJOR EDGEMAN 12/13 Northumberland Fusiliers came up to reconnoitre the line during the morning whilst Lieutenants & O.R.'s of same regiment arrived in the evening. They were sent to Companies to whom they were to relieve. The vicinities of the Company in support of Battalion H.Q. were shelled with a few gas shells during the earlier part of the night. The enemy's retaliation to our practice barrages was not heavy or strong throughout the day. "B" Company sent out a patrol who found 2 hostile Machine guns along TURNER'S AVENUE, about 200 East of Company H.Q. They were soon driven off the place. "D" Company patrolled the whole of their front throughout the night, but did not get into touch with any of the enemy. A finally great night. Casualties: Nil. 2nd Lt. P.A. Curtois rejoined from hospital (wounds)	H.C.C. Appendix 16

Army Form C. 2118.

WAR DIARY
or
INTELLIGENCE SUMMARY.
(Erase heading not required.)

Instructions regarding War Diaries and Intelligence Summaries are contained in F.S. Regs., Part II and the Staff Manual respectively. Title pages will be prepared in manuscript.

Hour, Date, Place	Summary of Events and Information	Remarks and references to Appendices
Trenches on RESTEL RIDGE East of POLYGON WOOD. OCTOBER 26.	The French & Fifth Army attacked to the North whilst the 5th Division attacked POLDERHOEK CHATEAU, the 7th Division afterwards attacking GHELUVELT to the South, a Chinese barrage was put up along 21st Divisional front. Zero hour 5.40 a.m. The enemy seems had observed his protective barrage along BECELAERE Road which he intensified on our guns opening whilst his barrage came down at 5.45 a.m. on Battalion HQ. which weakened at 6.20 a.m. finally dying away 7.30 a.m. A very wet morning. The signal signifying capture of POLDERHOEK CHATEAU was seen at 6.50 a.m. A prisoner of the 9th Grenadier Regiment gave himself up & was sent down as quickly as possible. News came from front line about 11.00.a.m that they had suffered no casualties from hostile barrage which had carried fallen behind them. At 5.0.p.m the 1/1/13 Northumberland Fusiliers arrived the relief proceeded satisfactorily the night being fine & enemy quiet. "A" Company had taken over at	H.C.C. Appendices. 16 " 18.

Army Form C. 2118.

WAR DIARY
or
INTELLIGENCE SUMMARY.
(Erase heading not required.)

Place	Date	Hour	Summary of Events and Information	Remarks and references to Appendices
Trenches on REUTEL RIDGE EAST of POLYGON WOOD	OCTOBER 26 Cont.d		The BUTTE de POLYGON and in support to the Brigade. News came that PEDERHOEK CHATEAU had been recaptured by the enemy. The relief was complete by 7.30 p.m. The Battalion has one company and in 2 shelters & dug-outs in western southern banks of ZILLIBEKE LAKE & in railway embankment 330 ̊ SouthWest of Lake by 9.30 p.m. Casualties O.R. 7 wounded	H.Q.C. H.Q.C.
ZILLIBEKE LAKE	27		Quiet day spent in cleaning the men up. Casualties O.R. 1 killed & wounded	H.Q.C.
"	28		Brigadier General C.G. Rawling C.M.G. C.I.E. Commanding 62nd Infantry Brigade was killed by a hostile shell at his H.Q. at HOOGE CRATER. The Battalion found a working party for R.E. A Company at the BUTTE de POLYGON was relieved by a company of the 10th Yorkshire Regiment. The relief being complete at 5.15 p.m. & the men being in their dug-outs in the railway embankment bends by 7.0 P.M. Casualties 1 wounded missing. Enemy shelled country of miles of containment with a long range gun in the morning otherwise a quiet day. A carrying party was found to carry bombs to 1st Hunts Regiment at the BUTTE de POLYGON. Major Infantry of the Battalion attended General Rawlings funeral at 2.0 p.m. at Hut Cemetry DICKEBUSCH	H.Q.C. Appendix 19. H.Q.C.
"	29			H.Q.C.
"	30		Quiet though wet day. Hon L.O. Croft East & DICKEBUSCH, Battalion left ZILLIBEKE LAKE at 3.30 p.m. arriving in camp at 5.0 p.m. the men were very cramped for room rather uncomfortable owing to kit not arrived. The following W.Os & men were awarded the Military Medal	H.Q.C. Appendix 22

WAR DIARY
or
INTELLIGENCE SUMMARY

Army Form C. 2118.

Place	Date	Hour	Summary of Events and Information	Remarks and references to Appendices
ZILLEBEKE LAKE	OCTOBER 30 cont'd		by the G.O.C. X Corps for bravery in the field :- 202312 Pte. C.J. Baker; 203415 Pte. S.J. Blaker; 205671 L/c. A. Lennon, 202110 Pte. H. Homewood, 205300 Pte. J. Capp. 201126 Pte. P.J. Kirvey, 2015-84 L/c. C.C. Clark, 203420 Pte. W/c Dunkley, 205844 L/c. A. Shipp 202094 Pte. W. T.C. Scearfield, 205735 Pte. A. Dix, 202559 Pte. B. W. Isalop, 202770 Sgt. F.C. Reid, 201346 Sgt. A. V. Glaze.	Appendix 20 " 21
CAMP "C" EAST of DICKEBUSCH.	31.		Day spent in cleaning up. CAPTAIN. N.TRON. M.C. E.I. & Mr. 2/Lt. 3/4 Queens was awarded the D.S.O. by His Majesty the King for bravery in the field.	N.C.O. Appendix 23 " 24

A.C. Cannon Major.
Commanding 3/4 "The Queens" Regt.

Appendix 21

No. 202312 Private Charles James Baker,
3/4th Bn. "The Queen's" (R.W.S.) Regt.

This man was a Company Stretcher Bearer throughout the period the Battalion was in the line East of POLYGON WOOD, viz. from October 2nd to October 7th, and was indefatiguable in his attendance to the wounded. From the commencement of the attack until the Battalion was relieved, almost without cessation he was out in the open under hostile shell and rifle fire, ministering to the wants of the wounded of his own and other units. He displayed great gallantry in carrying severely wounded men on his back to a place of safety, and by his efforts undoubtedly saved the lives of many men. Although this man has no outstanding deed of gallantry to his credit, his work far outshone that of any other N.C.O. and man in the Battalion.

I consider this man's fine example of personal bravery and unselfish devotion to duty under such terrible conditions well worthy of official recognition.

No. 200094 Sergeant William Tamlin Grant Swarfield,
3/4th Bn. "The Queen's" (R.W.S.) Regt.

This N.C.O. took command of a platoon on his officer becoming a casualty in the attack on Oct. 4th East of POLYGON WOOD, during which he displayed great coolness and continually rallied his men, who were shaken by the heavy hostile bombardment. For 24 hours he held an advanced post in the front of the second objective, thus keeping up communication with the Brigade on the left, and was also instrumental in beating off an enemy counter attack. This N.C.O. did much to keep up the spirits of his men in adverse and difficult conditions, and I consider his conspicuous gallantry and zealous devotion to duty well worthy of official recognition.

No.205735 Private Albert Dix,
3/4th Bn. "The Queen's" (R.W.S.)Regt.

This man was a Company runner during the operations from October 2nd to October 7th inclusive, East of POLYGON WOOD. He continually carried messages of tactical importance to Battalion Headquarters through the enemy barrage after the attack on October 4th. He was wounded on the night of Oct. 4th, but proceeded to carry out his duties, always cheerfully taking messages over the open through hostile shell and rifle fire, never failing to deliver the message to the assigned recipient. On the night of relief, viz. Oct. 7th, it was solely due to his efforts that his Company was guided from the line successfully. I consider this man's fine example of unselfish endurance and gallant devotion to duty well worthy of official recognition.

No.205459 Private Bertie William Gallop,
3/4th Bn. "The Queen's" (R.W.S.) Regt.

East of POLYGON WOOD on the night of Oct. 4th a man was heard calling for assistance from a shell hole about 50 yards away, in the open; this man volunteered to go to his aid leaving his place of safety regardless of danger; he found a wounded man buried by a shell explosion; he dug the man out and dressed his wounds. He then went back to the Regimental Aid Post to guide two bearers, and saw the wounded man safely carried away. He was out more than one and a half hours on his errand of mercy amidst continual shell fire. I consider this man's unselfish act of gallantry well worthy of official recognition.

No.200770 Sergeant Frank Reid,
3/4th Bn. "The Queen's" (R.W.S.)Regt.

On October 4th, East of POLYGON WOOD, all his officers had become casualties during the attack, and this N.C.O. took command of the Company. At the first objective he superintended the consolidation, reorganising the men and arranging them into the proper posts. Throughout the five days during which the Battalion was in the line, he always set a fine example of personal bravery and cheerful disposition under the most adverse circumstances. I consider this N.C.O's zealous devotion to duty and outstanding display of iniative, upon his officers becoming casualties well worthy of official recognition.

No.201348 Sergeant Albert Victor Glaze,
3/4th Bn. "The Queen's" (R.W.S.)Regt.

East of POLYGON WOOD on October 4th, upon his officer becoming a casualty this N.C.O. took command of the platoon, and successfully led the men to the first objective, where he consolidated his position with great skill. Throughout the whole period he was indefatiguable in his efforts in collecting stragglers and rallying men when they became at all shaken by the intense shell fire. He was untiring in his efforts to see that the consolidation was complete, superintending the digging with complete disregard to enemy fire. He set a fine example of coolness and courage throughout the whole operation, and I consider his gallant behaviour and zealous devotion to duty well worthy of official recognition.

No.201126 Corporal Frederick James Linsey,
3/4th Bn. "The Queen's" (R.W.S.) Regt.

This N.C.O. was continually with the pack animals taking rations to the line, East of POLYGON WOOD, and always displayed the greatest courage and devotion to duty in getting the convoy through the heaviest shell fire. It was solely due to his efforts that rations arrived every night at the assigned dump. On October 6th, especially, he showed the greatest coolness and perseverance under abnormal conditions in getting the pack animals to the MOUND North of POLYGON WOOD by daylight, when he displayed great disregard of personal safety in helping to extricate several animals who had become deeply embedded in the mud amidst heavy enemy shelling. I consider this N.C.O's fine example, devotion to duty and carelessness of danger well worthy of official recognition.

No.201584 Private (L/Corporal) Charles Cecil Clark, 3/4th Bn. "The Queen's" (R.W.S.) Regt.

This N.C.O. was in charge of a portion of the Battalion Carrying Party; he continuously showed great devotion to duty, in reaching Battalion Headquarters, East of POLYGON WOOD with rations amidst heavy shell fire. He never failed to deliver his load at the proper destination. On the night of Oct. 5th, the party was under especially heavy shell fire in GLENCORSE WOOD, but this N.C.O. successfully led his party through the barrage and carried out his mission with only one casualty. The Carrying Party all agree that it was only this N.C.Os. determination to succeed, his personal bravery, and cheerful disposition, which enabled them to carry out their tasks.

I consider this N.C.Os. personal gallantry and zealous devotion to duty well worthy of official recognition.

No.205420 Private Horace Cecil Dunkley 3/4th Bn. "The Queen's" (R.W.S.) Regt.

This man was a Company runner and set a fine example of devotion to duty throughout the past operations East of POLYGON WOOD, always cheerfully carrying out any orders given him, and fearlessly bearing any message to its proper destination without the slightest delay, despite hostile shell and rifle fire. On Oct. 4th he carried a wounded man on his back through the POLYGON BROOK, although this was one of the enemy's barrage lines, and the water was above his knees. I consider this man's zealous devotion to duty a great act of gallantry and well owrhhy of official recognition.

No.206110 Private Harry Homewood, 3/4th Bn. "The Queen's" (R.W.S.) Regt.

East of POLYGON WOOD on October 4th, a stretcher bearer having become a casualty this man volunteered to perform his duty and went out in the open under exceptionally heavy shell fire to the help of a wounded man whose hurts he dressed and carried on his back to a place of safety. On the following days he was unflagging in his energies in dressing the wounded, superintending their removal to the aid post. On Oct. 6th when the platoon was without rations this man volunteered to fetch same which he successfully did despite the hostile barrage behind the line. Throughout he set a fine example of zealous devotion to duty and disregard of self when others had to be considered and in my opinion he is worthy of official recognition.

No.20550 Private John Capp,
3/4th Bn. "The Queen's" (R.W.S.) Regt.

East of POLYGON WOOD on the night of Oct. 7th the line was subjected to a heavy hostile bombardment causing several casualties amongst the garrison of the trench. As the Battalion was to be relieved that night it was most essential that the wounded should be cleared as soon as possible, despite the enemy's barrage. Private Capp made two journeys to the rear each time returning with a stretcher, thereby greatly aiding the removal of the casualties. I consider this man's act of gallantry well worthy of official recognition.

No.206844 Private (L/Corporal) Arthur Thipp,
3/4th Bn. "The Queen's" (R.W.S.)Regt.

This L.C.O. was severely wounded at the commencement of the attack on the morning of Oc. 4th East of POLYGON WOOD but he carried on with his duties as a Company runner, and was invaluable in his efforts in directing men who had lost themselves in the dark, towards the Company's objective. He continued to carry messages throughout the day amidst heavy shelling and sniping of the enemy, and only ceased his efforts when the effects of his wound rendered him too weak to proceed with his duties. I consider this N.C.O's. fine example of gallantry and unselfish devotion to duty deserves official recognition.

No.205413 Private Sydney John Blake,
3/4th Bn. "The Queen's" (R.W.S.) Regt.

This man was a Company stretcher bearer during the whole five days the Battalion was in the line East of POLYGON WOOD and fearlessly attended the wounded, careless of his own personal safety. After the attack on the morning of the 4th October he remained in the open for several hours dressing the wounded, despite hostile shell and rifle fire. On October 5th he went out alone 200 yards in advance of the front line amongst hostile machine gun and rifle fire to a wounded man, whom he dressed and carried to the trench on his back.

I consider this man's fine example of bravery and carelessness of personal safety well worthy of official recognition.

No.205471 Private (L/Corporal) Arthur Victor Lemon,
3/4th Bn. "The Queen's" (R.W.S.) Regt.

East of POLYGON WOOD on the morning of October 4th, during the attack, and enemy machine gun and crew were holding up part of the line, and were proving a great obstacle to the advance; this N.C.O. quickly got four men together and on his own iniative attacked the hostile machine gun, killing the crew and destroying the weapon, and so allowing the assault to proceed. I consider this act of gallantry and outstanding example of iniative and dash set by this N.C.O. well worthy of official recognition.

Appendix 1.

OPERATION ORDER No. 9.   Copy No. 4.
by Lieut.Col.K.A.Oswald.
Commanding O X E N.

Map.Sheet GHELUVERT.   2.10.17.

1. The Battalion will relieve the 8th Leicester Regt. in the front line tonight.

2. The Battalion will leave present quarters at 6.15 p.m. in following order:- Bn.H.Q's.Coy. - "A" - "D" - "B" - "C" Coys. Movement will be by half Platoons at 75 yds.interval.

3. Guides from 8th Leicester Regt. will meet Battalion at CLAPHAM JUNCTION at 7.45 p.m.

4. Each Coy., including H.Q's. Coy. will take 16 Petrol Tins of water up to Front Line. Men have been detailed from Carrying Parties to accompany respective Coys. All Petrol Tins must be returned to Bn. H.Q's. front line by 8 p.m. 3.10.17.

5. Each man will carry iron ration and 2 days' rations.

6. The 62nd Machine Gun Section will accompany "C" Coy. Surplus Coy. Officers with Bn.H.Q's., Coys. reserve L.G. and teams of "B" & "D" Coys. will accompany Bn.H.Q's. Coy., those of "C" & "A" Coys. will accompany "C" Coy.

            (Sgd.) V.F.Samuelson,
            Captain & Adjutant.
            O X E N.

Issued Verbally at 5 p.m.
 to Representatives of Coys.
Copy No. 1 Filed.
 " " 2 BOLT.
 " " 3/4 War Diary.

SECRET.　　　　　　　　　　　　　　　　　　　　　　　　COPY No. 15.

Appendix 2

OPERATION ORDER No. 10 BY
LIEUT-COLONEL K.A.OSWALD,
COMMANDING 3/4th Bn. "THE QUEEN'S" (RWS) REGT.

Ref.Map 1/10000.　　　　　　　　　　　　　　　　　　2nd. Oct., 1917.
　　RECELAERE.
　　(ed 1a)

1. INFORMATION.

The 62nd. Inf. Brigade has been ordered to attack and consolidate the objectives as detailed at an hour and date to be notified later.

2. INTENTION.

The attack to capture and consolidate the first objective will be carried out by this Battalion. The K.O.Y.L.I. on the right and the S. Stafford Regt. on the left will attack at the same time.

3. DISPOSITION.

The Battalion will attack on a three Company front, each with one platoon up as follows -
　　　　　　　　　"A" Company on the Right
　　　　　　　　　"B"   "   in the Centre
　　　　　　　　　"D"   "   on the left, each on a frontage of 85 yards.

"C" Company will be in Reserve and follow the left centre of the attack. JUMPING OFF details will be issued later.

The Reserve Lewis Gun and team of "A" & "C" Companies will move with "C" Company during the advance. "B" & "D" Companies with Battalion H.Q.

One Section of 62nd. M.G. Coy. will move with the Reserve Coy. one sub-section on each flank.

Two Mortars of 62nd. T.M.Battery will move in rear of the Reserve Coy.

4. FORMATION.

The normal formation will be adopted, the Battalion advancing at a maximum depth of 60 yards - re-adjusting to normal distances after 250^x have been covered.

5. BARRAGE.

Rate of Barrage will be notified later.

6. OPERATION.

As soon as the objective has been reached by the leading Companies - posts will be pushed forward - and the line will be consolidated by formation of Platoon posts either in existing trenches or by connecting up shell holes which will be formed into a continuous line at night. Rear lines must be made as strong as possible.

Os. i/c. Machine Gun and T.M. Sections will at once barrage and assist in the dislodgement of any enemy counter attack which may have penetrated our lines or threaten them and also assist in the reduction of strong points. In the event of the attack on the second objective being successful the line of Judge Trench will be consolidated as a Reserve Line with the M.Gs. on the flanks. These guns are then liable to be sent forward. This Battalion will commence to consolidate this line as soon as they have captured it.

The Battalion will be reorganised during consolidation.

On relief by one Company from the 10th Yorks Regt. and 12/13th Northumberland Fus., the Battalion will withdraw as follows.

"A" & "B" Coys. to JETTY WARREN and "C" & "D" Coys. to about J 10 d.8.8. supporting 12/13th N. Fusiliers and 10th Yorks Regt respectively.

OPERATION ORDER No. 17
by Major H.G.CANNON, M.C.,
Commanding O X E N.

Copy No. 10

Map Ref. Sheet 28.   28th October, 1917.

1. The 62nd Inf.Bde. will be relieved by the 64th Inf.Bde. between 30.10.17 and 1.11.17.

2. The Battalion will leave present quarters tomorrow 30th instant and proceed by route march to Camp "C" H.36.c. as under:-

    "C" Coy. 3.30 p.m. - "A" Coy. 3.35 p.m. - "B" Coy. 3.40 p.m. "D" Coy. 3.45 p.m.
    Bn.Headquarters' Coy. will move with "B" Coy., O.C. "B" Coy. issuing necessary instructions. Movement will be by Companies.

3. Route:- SHRAPNEL CORNER - WITHUS CAPE - KRUISSTRAATHOEK X ROADS and hence by guides to Camp.

4. O.C.Coys. will each detail their C.Q.M.Ss. and five men, H.Q.Coy. 1 N.C.O. and 4 men to report to Lieut. CARTER at Transport Lines by 9 a.m.

5. Lieut. CARTER will proceed with above party and take over the camp from the 9th K.O.L.I. and allot all tents, bivouacs etc. He will send to Cross Roads H.30.d.2.2 one man of above party per Coy. except B.H.Q. to guide Companies to Camp from X Roads at 4.15 p.m.

6. All dug-outs must be left thoroughly clean.

7. O.C.Transport will detail 2 Limbers to convey Officers' kits to Camp. One will convey "A" & "C" Coys., and one B.H.Q's. "B" & "D" Coys. A guide from Transport Lines will report at respective Coy. H.Q's. at about 12.45 a.m. stating where the limber is, and kits will be conveyed there. Coy. L.G.Limbers will come up at 2.30 p.m. and a guide from Transport Lines will report respective Coy. H.Q's., reporting place of limber, when Lewis Guns and Coy. Officers' Canteens will be sent.
    Each Coy. will detail an escort of 1 N.C.O. and 2 men.
    Horses for cookers and T.Cart will report at 2.30 p.m. Teas and Dixies will be sent on Cookers. Coy. Cooks will accompany cookers.
    Coy.Commanders' chargers will be sent up at 3.20 p.m.

8. Packs will be carried and each man will be issued with a full oil bottle if possible.

9. Acknowledge.

Issued by Orderly Sergeants at 7 p.m.   Captain &
        29.10.17.   Adjutant   O X E N.
Copy No. 1 Filed.
  "   " 2/5 Coy.Commanders.
  "   " 6 62nd Inf.Bde.
  "   " 7 Transport Officer.
  "   " 8 Q.M.
  "   " 9/10 War Diary.

Appendix 23

Copy of Xth CORPS ROUTINE ORDER No. 1834
dated 29th October 1917.

1834 IMMEDIATE AWARDS.

Under authority granted by His Majesty the King, the Field Marshall Commanding-in-Chief has awarded the following decorations to the undermentioned officers and other ranks for gallantry in the field on the dates stated :-

THE DISTINGUISHED SERVICE ORDER.

The Rev. M. TRON, M.C., Army Chaplains Dpt. attached R. W. Surr. Regt. .... 2 - 7.10.17.

---------oOo---------

Appendix 8.

Narrative of operations of the 62nd Infantry Brigade from October 2nd to October 7th, 1917, including the battle of POLYGON BEEK on Oct. 4th.

On the night of 2/3rd October, 1917, the 3/4th "Queen's" (R⁺S) R. took over the front held by the 8th Leicester Regt. East of the POLYGON WOOD. The previous day a powerful counter attack by the enemy had bent the line back on the right to a depth of 250 yards, which position was taken over by the 64th Infantry Bde., under Brigadier General HEADLAM. On the left of the 62nd Infantry Bde. was the 91st Infantry Bde. under Brigadier General PELLY.

The 21st Division on the right and the 7th Division on the left were ordered to attack and capture the enemy's defensive system on the BROODSEINDE-BECELEARE RIDGE.

The Objectives of the 62nd Infantry Bde. were as follows :-

1st Objective: The road from J 11 a 60 55 to J 11 a 85 30.
2nd Objective: The line J 11 d 65 75 - J 11 b 95 15 - J 12 a 1.5. the total depth to be captured being about 1200 yards.

On the night 3/4th October the remaining Battalions moved up to their assembly positions on the Eastern edge of POLYGON WOOD, which in daylight were in full view of the enemy. The night was dark with occasional drizzle.

The configuration of the ground and the natural obstacles gave every advantage to the defenders.

The place of assembly was thirty feet below the first objective and in full view of the enemy. Three streams separated the opposing forces. Each stream ran through soft and boggy ground 50 yards in width. This ground had been churned by the continuous shelling to an almost impenetrable morass. Scrub covered the slopes of the small spurs and this was all heavily wired. About 50 yards to the East of the POLYGON BEEK and again to the East of JETTY WARREN powerful concrete blockhouses, some containing three compartments, and each provided with loopholes, and manned by garrisons of 20 or 30 with machine guns and trench mortars commanded all approaches.

4' to 5' deep trenches were sited on all the prominent positions. The beds of the streams were swept by machine gun fire from CAMERON COVERT AND POLDERHOEK CHATEAU. As seen in daylight after the attack the

- 2 -

position appeared impregnable.

The original plan of attack was as follows :-

1st Objective to be taken by the 3/4 "Queen's" (RWS)R. and the 2nd Objective by the 12/13 Northumberland Fusiliers on the right and the 10th Bn. Yorkshire Regt. on the left with the 1st Lincolnshire Regt. in close reserve.

During the move to the assembly positions the 10th Yorks Regt. was caught in two heavy barrages, one in GLENCORSE WOOD and the other when passing BLACK WATCH CORNER, thereby becoming disorganized and suffering heavy casualties, owing to which this Battalion did not arrive at its assembly position until 15 minutes after the hour ordered. In the meantime the C. O. 1st Lincoln R., acting on alternative orders, issued by the Brigade, moved his Battalion from the Reserve to the position which was to have been occupied by the 10th Yorks R. The 10th Yorks R. on arrival took up the position of Reserve. Heavy shelling continued over the whole area during the night and the moving troops were silhouetted against the light of the burning ammunition dumps. Under cover of the darkness guiding tapes were put out by the three leading Battalions and posts were pushed forward in to the POLYGON BEEK to prevent the enemy observing the assembly of the troops.

At 5.30 a.m. the enemy put down a heavy barrage behind our front line, but, owing to the three leading Battalions keeping right up to one another and occupying a total depth of less than 200 yards, casualties were few.

At ZERO hour, 6.0 a.m. the attack commenced under cover of a very heavy artillery and machine gun barrage.

The leading Battalions advanced in mass.

The immediate obstacle of the POLYGON BEEK with its mud and tangled wire was found so difficult to negotiate that the artillery barrage (which for the first 200 yards moved at the rate of 100 yards in 4 minutes and afterwards, up to the first objective, at 100 yards in every 6 minutes) crept away from the advancing troops and was not regained until JETTY WARREN was reached.

A few mud mats and trench-boards which had been brought up with great difficulty and placed in position, considerably helped the crossing of the troops and more particularly of the lightly equipped leading platoons. The 12/13 Northumberland Fusiliers and the 1st Lincoln Regt. followed close on the heels of the 3/4th "Queen's" while the 10th Yorks Regt. moved into the vacated front line.

Several unsuspected and well hidden concrete emplacements on the Eastern Bank of the POLYGON BEEK, each manned by garrisons of 20 to 30 men and 3 machine guns, immediately the barrage had passed opened fire on the advancing troops, causing many casualties. The offensive spirit of the 3/4th "Queen's" in this, their first fight, was beyond all praise and their recent hard training enabled them to instinctively work round these "mebus" and reduce them with skill and rapidity.

c The capture of these powerful concrete shelters, in all of which the enemy put up a determined resistance, were amongst the brightest features of the day, and were only accomplished by previous good training, absolute determination to win, and a complete disregard of self. The stubborn resistance of the line as a whole, despite the numbers of Germans who fled to the rear, the heavy machine gun fire up the valley from the right, and the natural and artificial obstacles encountered, combined, had so delayed the leading troops that the artillery barrage was now 250 yards away.

Lieut.Col. EVANS, Commdg. 1st Lincoln R. and Lieut.Col. DIX, Comdg. 12/13th Northd.Fus. realising the seriousness of the situation closed up their Battalions still tighter.

The O.C. 1st Lincoln Regt. passed his two leading Companies through the Northern Companies of the "Queen's", scrambled across the bog of JETTY WARREN, and rushed the first objective, killing large numbers of the enemy.

The Northumberland Fusiliers on the right, ably backed up the "Queen's", reached JUDGE TRENCH at the same time.

The trenches which were found to be in very fair condition were filled with the troops of the XIXth Reserve Division, which Division had just been brought over from the RIGA front.

The bayonet was freely used and large numbers of the fleeing enemy were shot with the rifle. Hand Grenades and P. Bombs cleared the mebus and rifle grenades the more distant shell holes. One mebus was apparently set on fire by a P bomb and burnt furiously, the whole garrison being shot as they fled or burnt to death before they could emerge.

The 12/13 N.Fs. had again to take part in a sever fight for a mebus about J 11 c 78, large numbers of Germans being killed and a few prisoners taken.

Prisoners were numerous and were estimated by 1 C.O. at 500, but the German dead far outnumbered these and were greatly in excess of our own casualties. It is worthy of record that no men desired to escort prisoners to the rear, their one and sole aim was to capture their objectives.

The artillery barrage which had halted 150 yards beyond, now contained a percentage of smoke shells. Here it remained for an hour and forty minutes, a barrier to any counter attack, and a wall of cover under which the "Queen's" energetically consolidated, and the 1st Lincolnshire Regiment and 12/13th Northumberland Fusiliers reorganized and prepared xxx to assume the attack on the 2nd objective. Direction up to now had been fairly well maintained, considering that the POLYGON BEEK, JUNIPER TRENCH, the almost impassable bog called JETTY WARREN and JUDGE TRENCH, all lay at entirely different angles from one another. Despite the fact that the situation must have been obscured by dust and smoke the fire of the enemy's machine guns from CAMERON COVERT and POLDERHOEK CHATEAU steadily increased in volume and caused great casualties in our ranks. While reorganising, Lt.Col.DIX, M.C. Comdg. the 12/13th Northumberland Fusiliers was shot as well as his four Company Commanders. The fire raked our ranks. Each of the three leading Battalions had now lost 40% of its effectives and no Battalion had more than 6 officers left. Gaps occurred in our line as the result of the obstacles encountered and the inequalities of the ground.

Units of the 64th Brigade on our right had merged into our line, while some of the Northumberland Fusiliers together with their two machine guns found themselves isolated in REPUEL and the cemetery.

The general situation at 6.30 a.m. on Oct. 4th was as follows:-
3/4 "Queen's" consolidating along the whole of the first objective less one Company digging in its immediate support. On the left in continuation of JUDGE TRENCH elements of the 1st South Staffords, on the right the KOYLI of the 64th Brigade. In advance on the left the 1st Lincolnshires forming for the attack on the 2nd objective. In the trenches on the right the Northumberland Fusiliers forming up for

the same purpose. It appeared that the 5th Division were held up at POLDERHOEK CHATEAU with the result that the 64th Brigade were being badly enfiladed by machine gun fire from this area. This in its turn effected the 12/13th who when the time came at 8.10 a.m. to advance on the 2nd objective, found their right flank in the air and at the same time were raked by intense machine gun fire from the chateau. After advancing 150 yards they dug in.

The 1st Lincolnshires on the left slightly protected by the curve of the spur and only subjected to indirect fire from the chateau, some machine gun fire from JUDGE COPSE and the two isolated mebus, and numerous snipers, esconsed in shell holes, obtained their final objective and consolidated. The line was not continuous but was sound in principle, with no dead ground uncovered. The Brigade had, owing to the inequalities of the ground, extended its flanks and had encroached into the 7th Div. area. The 3/4th "Queen's" had thrown back a defensive flank on the right in expectation of a counter attack from REUTEL. While the attack was proceeding the enemy heavily shelled POLYGON WOOD and the back areas.

No outstanding incident took place until 3.0 p.m. when the enemy was seen massing behind CAMERON COVERT preparatory to counter attacking the 5th Division. A successful pigeon message despatched by Lieut. FROST of the 3/4th "Queen's" brought down such an accurate and heavy artillery fire on the spot as to disperse the whole force, at the same time causing heavy casualties.

It is impossible to estimate with any accuracy the numbers of the enemy killed during the morning's fight, but the numbers were far in excess of anything witnessed by the Brigade in the Battle of the SOMME. One Battalion alone captured 8 heavy machine guns, 7 light guns, 5 Trench mortars and 5 Granatenwerfers.

The night of the 4/5th October up to 10 a.m. on the 5th passed quietly. From thence onward, and until the Brigade was relieved on the morning of October 8th by the 22nd Infy.Bde. the front line and supports were shelled heavily at intervals.

Two weak counter attacks were crushed at their inception by the artillery and machine gun fire.

During the night of the 4/5th October, the 6th Leicester Regt. (Lt.Col.STEWART) relieved the 1st Lincoln Regt. and the 12/13th Northumberland Fus. in the front line. The two relieved Battalions moved to the area of ZILLEBEKE LAKE. The 3/4th "Queen's" remained in close support, and the 10th Yorks R. in reserve.

On the night of thr 5/6th the 6th Leicesters pushed forward posts and to all intents and purposes occupied the ground of what was intended to be the final objective on October 4th.

The operations from October 3rd to October 8th had cost the 62nd Infantry Brigade heavy casualties, 74 officers out of 86 who had gone into action and 1279 other ranks. Despite their losses, the scarcity of food and water (the carrying of which was almost stopped by the continuous enemy barrage), and the wet, the "morale" of all ranks remained extremely high. The victory had been a complete one, and the enemy signally defeated.

The report on the excellent work carried out by the Machine Guns and the Light Trench Mortar Battery is attached as an appendix.

Incidents of treachery, lessons learnt, and remarks on enemy action are also attached as an appendix.

Captain Mazzini Tron, M.C., C.F.
att. 3/4th "Queen's" (R.W.S.) Regiment.

This Officer, throughout the past operations East of POLYGON WOOD from Oct. 2nd to Oct. 7th continually performed acts of great gallantry. On October 2nd, when the Battalion was forced to take cover during the hostile bombardment on the way up to the line, he fearlessly exposed himself tending wounded. On Oct. 3rd, whilst the Battalion was in the line, he carried out the duties of the Medical Officer, who had been wounded. His cheerful demeanour worked wonders in keeping up the spirits of all officers and men whilst assembling prior to the attack on October 4th, in which he took part for the purpose of dressing the wounded, which duty of mercy he performed continuously. The arrival of rations to the Battalion on Oct. 4th was solely due to his unflagging energy and cheery optimism in guiding the carrying party. He was always regardless of his own personal safety when there were any wounded who required his attention. Not only did he tend the living but also the dead, as every man of the Battalion was decently buried by him, in addition to all those of other units who were lying around the Battalion's sector. His unceasing efforts under conditions of bombardment, rain and darkness were of immense value in keeping up the spirits of the men. I consider this officer's zealous devotion to duty, unremitting attention to the wounded, care for the bodies of the dead, personal example of bravery and cheerful disposition in such difficult and adverse circumstances merit him to be a recipient of the highest award.

For further details please see evidence attached.

This Officer has already been recommended for a bar to his Military Cross.

APPENDIX 1.   REPORT ON MACHINE GUNS.

No. 2 Barrage Group took up its position on September 30th at J.9.d.9.2 where the position was selected by the Battery Commander. The Sub-Battery Commander superintended the supply of 100,000 rounds of ammunition, which was conveyed up with great success on limbers and mules via GLENCORSE WOOD, and BLACK WATCH CORNER. By the afternoon of October 3rd the Battery was all ready for action with S.O.S. lines laid and gun orders issued. The S.O.S. signals were answered by all guns with great promptitude and even when most of the officers became casualties, the section N.C.Os. in most cases carried on their duties efficiently. The mobile guns detailed to be attached to each Battalion in the attack, found some difficulty in joining their Battalions at the forming up position, owing to the nature of the ground, and it was found difficult to keep touch in the attack. Two guns attached to the 12/13th Northumberland Fus. lost direction and found themselves in front of the 64th Inf.Bde., their positions, however, proved so favourable both for defensive and offensive action that it was retained. Excellent work was done by these two guns. The two guns attached to the 10th Yorks Regt. had their officer wounded and lost direction, finding themselves in the 7th Div. area on the left of our Brigade, where they proved of little use. Of the four guns attached to the 3/4th "Queen's" one was destroyed, two of the remainder were pushed forward on the right flank, and one was brought back to the spur in order to get a greater volume of fire.

The 5 sappers and the A...M.G.orderlies rendered most valuable service to the Company in spite of the difficult nature of the operations and proved very useful in every way.

In the case of the carrying parties it was found that a greater portion of full N.C.Os. would have rendered these parties much more efficient.

Appendix 4

COPY No. 8.

OPERATION ORDER No. 11 BY
CAPTAIN V.F.SAMUELSON
COMMANDING "OXEN" IN FRONT LINE.

Map Ref. Sheet GHELUVELT.   7.10.17.

1. The Battalion will be relieved in the front line to-night by 1 Coy. 1st. R.W.Fusiliers in close support JUDGE TRENCH ("A" & "B" Coys)

2. "C" & "D" Coys. & Bn. H.Q. will vacate their trenches at 10 p.m. or any time after the Company Commander considers it fit, owing to the Counter Battery work, and will move direct to CLAPHAM JUNCTION reporting to Lieut. H.W.CARTER who will act as guide to ZILLEBEKE.
"A" & "B" Coys will move direct to CLAPHAM JUNCTION on completion of relief and report to the Adjutant.

3. Coys. will move by half Coys. at 50 yds. interval.

4. All Pigeons and empty Baskets will be taken with Coys. and handed to Lieut. CARTER tomorrow morning.

5. All rations, water, maps, aeroplane photos, S.A.A. and other stores will be handed over.
Immediately on completion of relief, Pouch Ammunition will be neatly dumped under cover for use by incoming unit with the exception of 1 Bandolier per man.
O.C. "C" & "D" Coys cannot comply with above, but will take everything with them.

6. Guides from Bn. H.Q. are reporting with these orders per Coy to guide them to CLAPHAM JUNCTION.

7. "C" & "D" Coy. Commanders will send a Company runner to Bn. H.Q. reporting vacation of trenches as soon as possible.

8. Efforts must be made to clear CLAPHAM JUNCTION by 5 a.m.

Copy No. 1. Filed.
        2/5. Coy. Commanders.
        6. BOLT
        7/8. War Diary.   Capt. & Adjutant,
                                                            "OXEN."

- 2 -

7. LIAISON.

Companies are responsible that Liaison and connection is kept between units and companies on either flanks. Companies in rear must keep in touch with those in front to be fully aware of the situation.

8. DRESS.

According to detailed instructions shovels will be carried by all with the exception of the leading Platoon.

9. COMPASSES.

All officers will take compass bearings on their final objectives. The Right being 85° grid and the Left 80° grid north.

10. COUNTER ATTACKS will be delivered on the initiative of support and local commanders immediately. Deployment position for reserves-formation and the order by which counter attack can be initiated must be understood by all.

11. RATIONS.

Every man will carry unexpended portion of Day's Rations and Iron Rations. All water bottles will be filled. Solidified Alcohol and Rum have been asked for.

12. Casualties.

All walking wounded will carry their rifle & equipment to Dressing Station, if possible.
Box Respirators must be carried by all wounded. Regimental Aid Post J 10.a.3.2.

13. Prisoners will be sent back in parties to limit escorts.

14. WATCHES will be synchronised under Battalion arrangements.

15. REPORTS to Battalion H.Q.

Issued at 7.15 a.m. by runner to
Copy No. 1 Filed
    2/6 Coy. Commanders.
       7 Fox.
       8 Dog.
       9 Bolt.
      10 MO.
      11 Lion
      12 Tigress
      13 Bear
  14/15 War Diary.

Capt. & Adjutant,
3/4th Bn. "The Queen's" (RWS) Regt.

Appendix 5

SECRET.
B.M.190.

12/13 Northd Fus.
1 Lincoln R.
10 York R.
3/4"The Queen's" (RWS) R.

Major General CAMPBELL, although severely regretting the heavy losses sustained by the battalions and units of the Brigade, heartily congratulates those who took part in the successful fight yesterday. The enemy was signally defeated although holding a commanding possession, protected by an almost impassable bog, and defended by concrete emplacements.

Despite your heavy losses you must, from necessity, hold on to the ground won for 4 or 5 days.

(Sgd.) G.M. Sharpe, for G.O.C.
Capt.,
Bde. Major,
62nd Infantry Bde.

5/10/17.

COPY.

Appendix 6

A. 1212/172.

To :-

    62nd. Infantry Brigade.
    64th Infantry Brigade.
    110th Infantry Brigade.

    I wish to convey to all ranks of your Brigade my most hearty congratulations on the great results obtained during the recent fighting.

    The difficulties which had to be overcome and the hardships to be endured clearly prove the magnificent spirit which animates all ranks of the division.

    It was only the splendid defence put up by the 110th Infantry Brigade on October 1st. that rendered possible the attack carried out by the 62nd. & 64th. Infantry Brigade on October 4th. The attack made by these two Brigades was largely instrumental in assisting to win what will probably prove to be the greatest and most important victory won by the British Army since the commencement of the War.

    No words of mine can rightly express the admiration I feel for the troops I have the honour to command.

                   (Sd) D.G.M. Campbell.
                      Major-General
              Commanding 21st Division.

H.Q., 21st Division.
12th October 1917.

Appendix 7

3/4th Bn. "The Queen's" (RWS) Reg.

A.   Narrative of Operations on October 4th,
East of POLYGON WOOD.

At 3.0 a.m. the Battalion commenced to assemble prior to the attack; the night was fairly dark and showery, whilst the hostile artillery was quiet. No difficulty whatever was experienced in concentrating the Battalion: the 2 white tapes which had been previously laid on the flanks of each Company frontage were found of inestimable value.

The dispositions of the regiment were as follows :-
     "A" Company on the right.
     "B"   "   in the centre.
     "D"   "   on the left.

They were drawn up in a line from J.10.b.1.0 to J.10.d.1.7, and each Company had a frontage of 85^X and a depth of 30^X, and were disposed in the normal formation of attack, viz. each Company on a one Platoon frontage.

"C" Company were in close support, and were formed up in one line of half platoons in file at ^{X} interval, their centre being directly behind the left of "B" Company.

2 reserve Lewis Gun Teams moved with "C" Company. There was one subsection of 62nd M.G.Co. on each flank of the Support Company, whilst 2 guns of the 62nd Trench Mortar Battery followed closely in rear of the centre.

The total depth of the battalion was 60^X, and the process of assembly was finished by 4.30 a.m.

At 5.30 a.m. the enemy put down a barrage over the assembly positions, to which our artillery retaliated; this continued until Zero hour, but the Battalion suffered no casualties.

At ZERO (6.00 a.m.) our barrage came down 150^X in front of our position, the assaulting Troops immediately advancing up to it; they found the "going" rather heavy, but could keep up to the barrage.

The first obstacle encountered was a line of concertina and barbed wire along the whole front, which patrols had been unable to entirely clear away, in addition the advance came under heavy enemy Machine Gun fire from the right at this juncture; both these obstructions were successfully negotiated with few casualties.

The POLYGON BEEK was then encountered, and proved a serious impediment to the advance, the Companies only possessing 4 mud mats and a few trench boards manufactured from the beds in enemy concrete "pill boxes", and these were found to be insufficient; the marsh and stream were crossed with some difficulty, but the barrage was lost for the time being, and some confusion resulted.

JUNIPER TRENCH was then assaulted, the wire in front forming no serious obstacle; many of the enemy emerged from its shelter, but owing to the darkness it was impossible to tell their intentions, and the majority were killed.

A hostile concrete fortress at J.10.d.3.6 put up some show of resistance, which was overcome by a party of bombers led by Lieut. A.B.Frost, and the structure set on fire, probably by 'P' Bombs.

The remaining portion of this German line of defence fell into our hands with no great difficulty.

The advance proceeded now well up to barrage again, and the first objective (RED LINE) was reached well up to time, the barrage halting showed the troops where it was.

JUDGE TRENCH was for the most part obliterated by artillery fire an advanced post of a Machine Gun Team in a shell hole showed fight, but were quickly overcome; the remainder of the enemy garrison surrendered or were killed.

The consolidation commenced immediately, 6 posts were dug along the RED LINE in front of which 4 Lewis Gun posts were formed, communication was established munication was established with the 1st Staffordshire Regiment on the left, and messages both by Company runners and pigeons were sent to higher authority informing them of the capture of the first objective.

The Support Company, part of which had previously reinforced the right Company for the assault of JUDGE TRENCH, were withdrawn 200^x in rear of RED LINE, where they consolidated a line of half platoon posts.

The remainder of 1st Lincolnshire Regiment and 12/13th Northumberland Fusiliers having gone through the line right up to barrage, the advance recommenced at 8.10 a.m. Owing to the number of officer casualties in the regiment certain posts of the Battalion who were not directly under the control of a commissioned rank went forward with the 2nd phase of the attack.

Two Companies of the Troops who had captured the BLUE LINE came back and took over the first objective, the "Queen's" withdrawing to JETTY WARREN, "A" & "B" Companies digging themselves in on the South Eastern edge, the former being on the right: "C" & "D" Companies consolidated a new position East of JUNIPER TRENCH, the former at J.10.d.6.8, and the latter around J.10.b.8.1, this manoeuvre being complete about 2.30 p.m.

"B" Company got into touch with 2 officers of the 12/13th Northumberland Fusiliers who were holding a concrete fortress with a party of 30 other ranks of all regiments, situated between JETTY WARREN and REUTEL Village. The enemy were seen massing for a counter attack around CAMERON COVERT, and a pigeon message was dispatched informing higher authority as to this concentration; in addition "C" Company was moved to form a defensive flank facing South East, whilst "B" Company were moved slightly forward to get a better field of fire commanding the threatened point. As soon as these movements had been completed our artillery barrage dispersed the hostile troops in question.

The enemy continued shelling the captured area with guns of all calibres, but no further infantry action took place.

Appendix 9

3/4th Bn. "THE QUEEN'S" (R.W.S) REGT.

Summary of Operations Oct. 1st to Oct.10th, 1917.

CASUALTIES.   A. Officers.

Oct. 2.	Capt. A.E.Mackenzie,R.A.M.C. att. 3/4"Queen's"		Wounded.
" 3.	Lieut. A. H. Dakin		do.
	Capt.V.Tron, M.C. C.F. att.3/4th "Queen's"		Wounded (at duty).
" 4.	Lieut. J.J.Brooke		Killed.
	Lieut. A.H.A.Cooper		do.
	Lieut. A.E.Barrow		do.
	Capt. F.M.Hepworth		Wounded.
	Capt. V.F.Samuelson		Wounded (at duty).
	Capt. C.G.Moss		Wounded.
	Lieut. A.E.Frost		Wounded (at duty).
	Lieut. A.H.Lovell		Wounded.
	Lieut. D.R.J.O'Connor		Wounded.
	2nd Lt. J.Ost		Wounded.
	2nd Lt. J.C.Davie		do.
	Capt. L.J.C.Vidler		Wounded (at duty).
	Lieut. S.J.Mason		do. do.
" 5.	Lt.Col. K.A.Oswald		Wounded.
	2nd Lt. C.A.Freestone		do.
" 6.	Lieut. P.A.Curtois		do.
" 8.	Lieut. G.A.Shaw		do.

TOTAL:- 3 Killed, 17 wounded (5 at duty).

B. Other Ranks.

Oct. 1.			1 Killed.			
" 2.			4 wounded.			
" 3.	1	do.	10	do.		
" 4.	49	do.	184	do.	19	missing.
" 5.	1	do.	20	do.	1	do.
" 6.	2	do.	8	do.		
" 7.	3	do.	12	do.	1	do.
" 10.	4	do.	3	do.		

TOTAL:- 61 Killed. 241 Wounded (6 at duty) 21 Missing.

PRISONERS.

200 German Officers, N.C.Os. and men were captured by the Battalion.

MATERIAL.

8 Heavy Machine Guns,
7 Light do. do.
5 Trench Mortars,
5 Granaten werfers,

were captured and destroyed by the Battalion.

INCIDENTS. Appendix 10.

1. A gross case of treachery occurred during the attack near a mebus in Jupiter Trench. A German officer surrendered and put up his hands. As Lieut. Cooper of the 3/4 "Queen's" went forward to take his surrender the German officer whipped out his revolver and shot Lieut. Cooper dead. Before he could do more harm the German's body was riddled with bullets from the rifles of the men who witnessed the treacherous act.

2. There was a great scarcity of stretchers and stretcher bearers. The present allotment of stretchers to a Battalion and trained carriers is much under what is wanted for the removal of the wounded in a modern battle. Stretcher bearers and stretchers from the Field Ambulance came up far too late. They should come on to the battlefield within an hour or two of the action. Although the Field Ambulance did excellent work the following day, many men doubtless died from exposure in the meantime.

3. The enemy fired continuously at the wounded and stretcher bearers when carrying wounded.

4. The total capture of material cannot be accurately determined, but it was about

        22 Heavy Machine Guns
        15 Light Guns
        15 T.Mortars
        and a few Grenatenwerfers.

These were by Brigade orders either destroyed or buried as they could not be removed to the rear.

5. On account of an inner compartment of a mebu reopening fire after the outer garrison had surrendered it was necessary to kill all the Germans in the post.

6. Bayonet work was impossible on the many Germans who fled to the rear as they ran without arms or equipment, but they offered good targets to the riflemen.

7. After the capture of the final objective one large howitzer, reported to be 6", continued to fire from 400 to 500 yards short, but caused no casualties.

8. Pigeons were found to be the only reliable means of communication for 12 hours after ZERO.

9. A single soldier escort of a batch of prisoners got bogged in POLYGON

BEEK, his prisoners worked with enthusiasm to ensure his rescue.

10. A private of the 1st Lincolnshire Regt. made three attempts to bayonet a German. Failing to make his bayonet penetrate the German had to be shot.

11. A German officer rushed at the Rev. TRON and nearly tore his coat from off his back. The padre who is a bit of a boxer, repeatedly struck the German in the face until they broke apart. Unslinging his glasses the German thrust them into the hands of the astonished clergyman, and tendered his surrender.

12. A small soldier of the 12/13th N.Fs. met a German hurrying round a mebu. A gutteral remark of the German was replied to with "Nong comprez", "From Riga" said the German, "To hell" said the Englishman pushing his bayonet into his opponent's body.

13. Further remarks by O.C. 3/4th "Queen's".

B. <u>Outstanding incidents which occured in the fighting on October 4th East of POLYGON WOOD.</u>

1. When the Battalion encountered hostile machine gun fire from the right flank before they reached the POLYGON BEEK, the small number of casualties is considered entirely due to the new formation of the attack, and if there had not been a slight check in the advance owing to the slight difficlty experienced going through the hostile wire, there would have been still fewer casualties.

2. The few mud mats and trench boards which were provided proved of inestimable value in crossing POLYGON BEEK, the sections which had none being left behind both by the barrage and their luckier comrade

3. The German concrete fortress at J.10.d.8.8 proved a greater obstacle than it might have done owing to the darkness and neighbouring sections being unable to see what was going on in front or on the flanks.

4. A hostile machine gun in front of JUDGE TRENCH was assaulted by a Lance Corporal and 4 men covered both by Lewis Gun and rifle grenade

5. The fact that the barrage halted was the only guide that the first objective had been reached.

6. The attacking lines of the 2nd objective appeared to be very thin in places, several of the Battalion posts which were commanded by

N.C.Os. only, on their own iniative advanced and filled the gaps, thus greatly strengthening the assault.

7. The process of "opening out" when No Man's Land had been crossed was found practically impossible owing to the bad light, the desire of all men to be as near the barrage as possible even though they were in the support Company, and the troops of the Battalions behind keeping close up during the whole advance.

8. The enemy massing near CAMERON COVERT appeared entirely oblivious of our presence on the high ground North of REUTEL and so fell an easy prey to our guns. Even if our artillery had not shelled this concentration, the commanding position of our two companies would have enabled them to cause very severe casualties amongst the attacking force.

Copy No.

Appendix H

OPERATION ORDER No. 12 BY
MAJOR H. C. CANNON, M. C.
COMMANDING 3/4th. Bn. "The Queen's" (RWS) Regt.

8th. Oct, 1917.

No. 1.

The Battalion will parade by Companies tomorrow at 12 noon to proceed to OUDEZDOM for entrainment.
Companies will march by half companies at 100 paces interval; two connecting files will be provided by each.
Dress, full marching order, less equipment dumped at Transport Field.
Headquarters will join their respective companies.
No rations will be issued.
The Battalion will detrain at EBBLINGHAM.

No. 2.

Breakfast will be provided at 7.a.m., and an early meal (midday rations) at 11 a.m.

No. 3.

The Drums will join the Battalion at Cross roads H 300.3.3. ANZAC CAMP.

No. 4.

Officers' valises will be dumped near Company Cookers at 4 p.m., for return by ration limber to Transport Lines.
Men of carrying party will pack surplus kit (overcoat, havresack, etc) in sandbags labelled at same time. All remaining stores, Lewis guns, Verey Pistols, etc, will be returned to Transport by limber leaving Zillibeke Lake at......

No. 5.

All trench shelters will be struck by 8.30 a.m. and dumped near Cookers.
All dug outs, lines must be left clean and a certificate to this effect rendered by Company Commanders.

No. 6.

Special efforts will be made to turn out the Battalion as smart as possible.

R B Bannerman
Lieutenant,
Ass. Adjutant of "OXEN"

ADMINISTRATIVE ORDERS.
8th October 1917.

No. 1.

Transport together with that of 10th Yorks Rt. will march off at 1.30 p.m., Oct. 9th.

No. 2.

Route to be followed LOCRE - BAILLEUL - STRAZELLE - HAZEBROUCK. Starting point LA CLYTTE cross roads.

No. 3.

Transport will halt for night in CAISTRE area. Representative on bicycle to be sent ahead to ascertain billeting accommodation for Area Commandt CAISTRE.

No. 4.

March will be resumed on Oct 10th at an hour to be arranged by Transport Officer.

No. 5.

100^X distance in line of march between each battns. transport.

No. 6.

Guides will be met on Oct. 10th at X roads 500^X N of C in SERCUS.

No. 7.

Limbers will carry down officers' Kits, Trench Stores, etc., early in evening Oct. 8th.

No. 8.

The 4 cookeers, water carts and open Mess cart will leave ZILLEBEKE LAKE at 11.45 a.m. sharp, 9th Oct.

No. 9.

One Limbered Wagon will be detailed to report at Zillebeke Lake at 8 p.m. to carry remaining surplus stores to transport.

R B Bannerman Lt.
Ass. Adjutant.
3/4th Bn. "The Queen's" (RWS) Regt,

Appendix 12

3/4th Bn. "The Queen's" (R.W.S.) Regiment.

The following N.C.Os. and men are recommended to
receive the Divisional Commander's Card
of Honour.
by Major H.C.Cannon, M.C. Condg. 3/4th "Queen's"
(R.W.S.) Regt.

1. No.205421 Pte T.C.French. A Company runner who at all times delivered his message through heaviest barrage.

2. No.207444 Pte C.W.Chew. When the team of a Lewis Gun had been all killed or wounded, rushed across the open, and again set up the gun in a commanding position.

3. No.2M574 L/Sgt. A. Tee. Took over duties of platoon sergeant on latter becoming a casualty, and carried on extremely well under very adverse conditions.

4. No.202963 Pte W.J.Adams. Did most excellent work with pack animals regardless of personal danger under heavy shell fire.

5. No.204864 Pte C.J.Burgess. Volunteered to go to aid of a wounded man in the open, and was wounded whilst carrying same to cover.

6. No.G/24948 Pte H.Brown. Set a fine example of physical endurance carrying on throughout the whole of October 4th although severely wounded at the outset.

7. No.202893 L/C A.G.Dimmer. Set a splendid example of endurance, remaining with the Company for 2 days, although wounded in the neck.

8. No.205439 Pte L.J.Wall. A determined runner, who always carried out his missions amidst the heaviest shell fire.

SECRET.　　　　　　　　　　　　　　　　　　　　　　　　　　Copy No. 12
　　　　　　　　　　OPERATION ORDER NO. 13
　　　　　　　　　　by MAJOR H.C.CANNON, M.C.,
　　　　　　　　　　Commanding O X E N.

Appendix 13

Map. Ref. Sheets
36a & 28.　　　　　　　　　　　　　　　　　　　　　　　19th Octr., 1917.

1. The 62nd Infantry Brigade will move by train to MICKMACK CAMP H.31.d West of DICKEBUSCH on October 20th.

2. Companies will pass the starting point C.3.d.2.6 at 4 p.m. in the following order:- H.Q.Coy., "B", "D", Band, "A", "C".
   Attached men of the 12/13th Northumberland Fusiliers and 1st Lincoln Regiments will move with "C" Coy.
   Dress:- Full Marching Order.

3. The Battalion Scouts and 4 Signallers per Company will join their Companies, and men detailed as H.Q. runners will join H.Q.Coy. before marching off.

4. Rations for October 21st and the unconsumed portion of 20th will be carried by each man. On no account are sandbags, or parcels to be carried.

5. The train leaves EBBLINGHAM Station at 6.59 p.m. and is due to arrive at DICKEBUSCH at 9.30 p.m. where a guide per Company will be met.

6. On the march from DICKEBUSCH to billets a distance of 200 yards will be maintained between Companies.

7. Acknowledge.

　　　　　　　　　　　　　　　　　　　　　　　　　　　　Lieut. & Acting
　　　　　　　　　　Adjutant, 3/4th Bn. "The Queen's" (RWS)Regt.

Issued by Orderly at
10.30 p.m.
Copy No. 1 Filed.
　"　2/5　All Companies.
　"　6　H.Q.Coy.
　"　7　T.O.
　"　8　Q.M.
　"　9　62nd Inf.Bde.
　"　10　M.O.
　"　11/12　War Diary.

ADMINISTRATIVE ORDERS ISSUED
IN CONJUNCTION WITH OPERATION
ORDER NO. 13.

19th October, 1917.

1. The Transport will move at 1.30 p.m. via HAZEBROUCK to EECKE.

2. The Transport Officer will send forward an advance party of 2 other ranks on bicycles to report to the Area Commandant EECKE to ascertain the whereabouts of accommodation.
These guides will meet the transport (at a spot) to be chosen by Lieut. E.W. Preston.

3. Baggage and supply waggons will move with the First Line Transport.

4. Three lorries for this Unit have been detailed to report at SERCUS Church at 9 a.m. The Quartermaster will send a guide to meet them at above time and place.

5. Blankets will be rolled in bundles of ten and clearly labelled with Coy. and Number of Platoon, and stacked at Quartermasters' Stores by 9.30 a.m.

6. Officers' kits will be stacked at Quartermaster's stores by 12 noon. Officers' mess kits will be stacked at Q.M. Stores by 1.30 p.m. sharp.

7. "D" Coy. will detail a party of 1 N.C.O. and 12 men to report to the Regimental Sergeant Major at 1 p.m. and a party of 1 N.C.O. and 8 men to report to the Quartermaster's stores at 10.0 a.m. for loading.

8. Dinners will be served at 12 noon sharp.

9. The Quartermaster will arrange for Cooks and camp kettles to travel on the lorries so that hot tea will be ready for the Battalion on arrival at billets. The remainder of the cooks march with their Companies.

Lieut. & Acting Adjutant.
3/4th Bn. "The Queen's" (R.W.S.) Regiment.

Appendix 14

OPERATION ORDER NO. 14.
by Major H.C.Cannon, M.C.
Commanding O X E N.

Copy No. 13

Oct. 21st, 1917.

1. The 62nd Inf.Bde. will relieve the 69th Inf.Bde. 23rd Division on the Left Sub-sector on the night of the 22/23rd October.

2. The 3/4 "Queen's" will relieve the 11th West Yorkshire Rgt. in the line, the left being J.5.b.3.3. and the right J.6.c.2.1.

3. "A" Coy. will be on the right, "C" Coy. on the left in the front line, "B" Coy. on the right "D" Coy. on the left in the support.

4. The Battalion will leave the present camp at 9.30 a.m. and march to ZILLEBEKE LAKE, where dinners will be served. From thence they will march to HOOGE CRATER arriving there at 4 p.m. where guides at the rate of 1 per platoon will be met.

5. Capt. A.T.Latham will be in command of the Battn. whilst on the way up to the line. He will report to the Commanding Officer at Battn. Headquarters J.4.d.95.55.

6. The codeword for "Relief complete" will be " T R O N ".

7. The Battn. will go up to the line in fighting order, the unexpended portion of the day's ration plus one day's ration being taken, each man carrying one Mills Bomb (No.23) and each rifle grenadier 5 No. 20 rifle grenades.

8. Packs, greatcoats, blankets, and soft caps, the latter in sandbags for each section, to be stacked outside the Orderly Room by 7.30 a.m.

9. The Battn. will march to ZILLEBEKE by Companies at 200 yards interval, from thence to the front line by platoons at 100 yards interval, with 200 yards between Companies. The Battn. will leave the present camp in the following order:-
H.Q., "A" Coy., "C" Coy. "B" Coy. "D" Coy.

10. The 35 N.C.Os. and men already detailed as Carriers will remain at ZILLEBEKE LAKE under the command of 2/Lt. S.Hall until he is relieved by 2/Lt. N.H.Sisterson. This party is under the command of Lt. Darcy 12/13th Northumberland Fusiliers.

11. O.C. "D" Coy. will detail 3 men to report to Sgt. hild before the Battn. moves off to act as Gas Guard at Batt.Headquarters.

12. O.C.Companies must be responsible that the feet of all their men proceeding to the trenches are thoroughly rubbed with either whale oil or anti frost bite grease before moving off.

13. The nucleus party already detailed will remain with the transport.

14. 4 Cookers and the medical cart will proceed with the Battn. as far as ZILLEBEKE only; the 4 Lewis Gun Limbers will meet the Battalion at JARGON CROSS ROADS J.7.d.9.2 at 4.30 p.m. O.C. Coys. will detail an N.C.O. and 3 men to go with their limbers to unload same, and await arrival of the Battalion.

15. In addition the Transport Officer will detail one Limber to carry Signalling stores, officers' kits, Mess kits, and Orderly Room material. This limber will proceed with those mentioned in para. 14. Sergt. Harding will detail 3 men to go with and unload same.

16. 2/Lt. S.Hall and 4 men of his party (one from each Coy.) will leave Camp at 8 a.m. and proceed to ZILLEBEKE to reconnoitre and find a suitable place for the Battalion to have dinner.

17. Whilst in the line O.C.Coys. must at all times do all that lies in their power to beat off hostile aeroplanes by means of Lewis Gun fire.

- 2 -

18. In addition to the bombs and rifle grenades mentioned in para 7 25 shovels will be carried per Coy. The Transport Officer will arrange that all Bombs and tools are taken to ZILLEBEKE where they will be distributed to the men.

19. All reports, with the exception of Evening Situation Report and Casualty Return will reach Battalion Headquarters before it is properly light in the morning.

20. Acknowledge.

                                      (Sgd.) A.H.John, Lieut.
                      Act.Adjutant   O X E N.

Issued by orderly at 10.30 p.m.

Copy No. 1 Filed.
  " " 2/5 Coy.Commanders.
  " " 6   H.Q.Coy.
  " " 7   Q.M.
  " " 8   T.O.
  " " 9   M.O.
  " " 10   62nd Inf.Bde.
  " " 11   10th Yorks.
  " " 12/13 War Diary.

AMENDMENT TO OPERATION　　　　　　　　　　　　　　Copy No. 13
ORDER NO. 14. by Major
H.C.Cannon, M.C. Commanding
O X E N.

21st Octr., 1917.

Reference Para. 4, "9.30 a.m." should read "10.30 a.m."

　　　　　　　　　　　　　　　　　　　　(Sgd.) A.H.John, Lieut.
　　　　　　　　　　　Act.Adjutant O X E N.

Issued by orderly at 10.30 p.m.
Copy No. 1 Filed.
　"　　"　2/5 Coy.Commanders.
　"　　"　 6 H.Q.Coy.
　"　　"　 7 Q.M.
　"　　"　 8 T.O.
　"　　"　 9 M.O.
　"　　"　10 62nd Inf.Bde.
　"　　"　11 10th Yorks.
　"　　"　12/13 War Diary.

Appendix. IV

DEFENCE SCHEME
for
Battalion holding left of Left Sub.- Sector.

Ref. Map
BECELAERE I A.

1. The front line will be held at all costs.

2. In the event of the enemy penetrating on either flank, Os. C. front Companies will drive them out by means of bombing squads covered by Rifle Grenade and Lewis Gun fire.

3. In the event of enemy penetrating the left of the front line, the Coy. in Close Support at J.5.d.1.9 will counter attack immediately on the iniative of its Commander, leaving 1 Lewis Gun and team to defend its late position.

    A communication trench is being dug on the South side of the valley in J.5.b under cover of which advance will be made.

4. In the event of the right of the front line being broken by a hostile attack, the Companies of TIGRESS around J.11.a.5.8. have been ordered to support the defence of OXEN'S front.

5. The Company in support at J.4.d.60.35 will not move from its present position unless ordered to do so by O.C. OXEN, in this emergency, the Company will move to new trench being dug through J.5.c.30.35 and hold that line at all costs, 1 Lewis Gun and team must be left to defend the late position.

6. Battalion Headquarters is situated at J.4.d.85 where the reserve S.A.A. and bomb dump is situated.

7. The Regimental Aid Post is at present situated at J.10.a.3.3, casualties should be taken to the SOUND from whence they will be guided to the Aid Post.

A.B. Frost
Lieut & A/Adj
OXEN

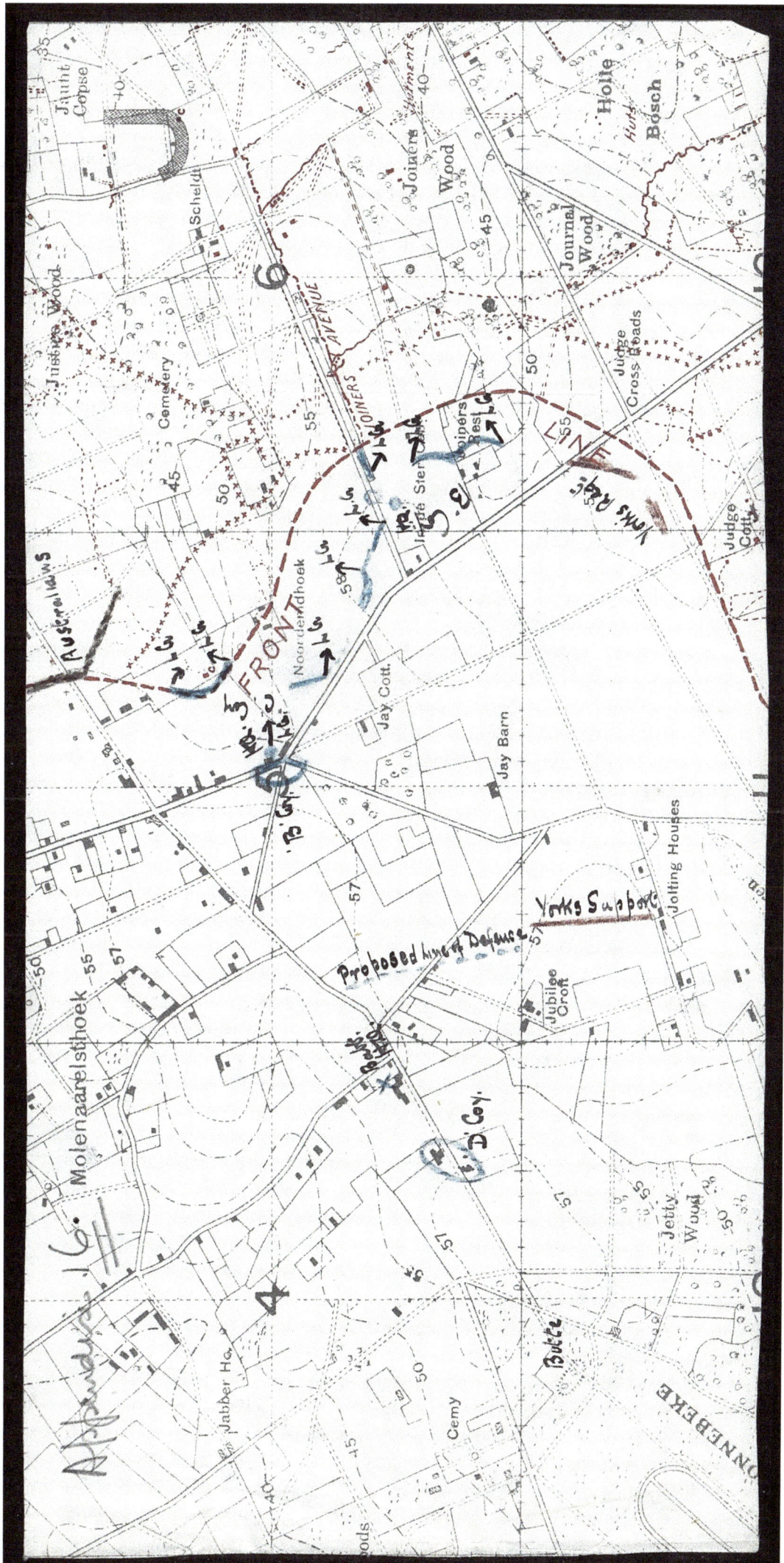

Appendix 17 B

RELIEF ORDERS BY
MAJOR H.C.CANNON, M.C.,
Commanding O X E N.   24.10.17.

1. **Relief.** Inter-Company relief will take place tonight, "B" Company relieving "A" on the right, and "D" Coy. relieving "C" on the left.
On completion of relief, "C" Company will move to "B" Company's present position in close support, and "A" Company to "D" Company's present position in reserve.

2. **Work.** O.C. "B" Company will continue "A" Company's work, i.e. connecting the posts on the S. side of the IN DE STER CABt. - SCHELDT road.
O.C. "D" Company will continue the communication trench on the South side of the valley at J.5.b.6.3.
O.C. "A" Company will continue the line of defence at J.5.c.5.7. - J.5.c.3.4.

3. **Rations.** O.C. "D" Company will arrange to pick up rations and water for "B" Company and dump them at present Headquarters. "B" Company will not move until their rations arrive at their present Headquarters.
O.C. "C" Company on completion of relief will send 1 N.C.O. and 9 men to Battalion Headquarters for rations and water. O.C. "A" Company will pick up their rations and water on their way to their new quarters.

4. **Move.** O.C. "D" Company will move from present quarters as soon as dark enough, provided enemy shelling allows.

5. **Lewis Gun.** O.C. "C" Company will send the Lewis Gun and team now at his Company Headquarters to "B" Company.

6. **Relief Complete.** O.C. Companies will report relief complete by runner at Battalion Headquarters - Code Word " P A D R E ".

7. **Acknowledgment.** Acknowledge.

24.10.17.
                                            A.B. Frost
                                                                    Lieut.
                                        /Adjutant, O X E N.

Appendix 18

RELIEF ORDERS No.2. by
MAJOR H.C.CANNON, M.C.,
Commanding O X E N.   25.10.17.

1. **Relief.** The Battalion will be relieved in the line by BEAR on the night of 26-27th October. "C" Company BEAR will relieve "B" Company OXEN, "B" Company BEAR will relieve "D" Company OXEN, "A" Company BEAR will relieve "C" Company OXEN, "D" Company BEAR will relieve "A" Company OXEN.

2. **Guides.** Four guides per Company and two from Headquarters under 2/Lt. Sheppard will meet BEAR at HOOGE CRATER at 4 p.m. 26th inst., and will lead relieving Battalion in by HELLES track in the following order:- Headquarters, "C" Company, "B" Company, "A" Company, "D" Company.

3. **Advance Party.** One Officer and two runners per Company of BEAR will arrive at Battalion Headquarters on the evening of the 25th and will be guided thence to their respective Companies. O.C.Companies will ensure that the runners of BEAR take every available opportunity of reconnoitring the route to Battalion Headquarters.

4. **Reserve Positions.** On completion of relief, "A" and "C" Companies will proceed to RAILWAY DUGOUTS I.21.d.4.6 whilst "B" and "D" Companies proceed to dugouts in the BUND, the West Bank of ZILLEBEKE LAKE I.21.b.1.5.

5. **Completion of Relief.** O.C.Companies will report completion of relief to Battalion Headquarters by runner. There must be no delay in doing this. Code word for relief "S M I T H".

6. **Move.** On relief Companies will proceed independently to new quarters in no larger or smaller bodies than 1 platoon.

7. **Move.** O.C.Companies are reminded that the relief must be carried out with all possible speed to ensure the Battalion missing hostile barrages. All their men must be ready to move away by 5 p.m.

8. **Handing Over.** All tools, maps, tape, piggeons, periscopes, bombs, rifle grenades, must be handed over to incoming Unit.

9. **Acknowledgment.** Acknowledge.

A.B. Frost
                                                    Lieut.
A/Adjutant,   O X E N.

Appendix 19

O. C. "A" Coy., O X E N.   27.10.17.

Map Ref. Sheet 28.

1. One Coy. 10th York Regt. will relieve you tomorrow, 28th inst. at BUTTE de POLYGONE.

2. On relief you will rejoin Battalion at ZILLEBEKE LAKE at I.21.b.1.5.

3. You will detail one guide per platoon to be at BUTTE de POLYGONE at 3.30 p.m. October 28th.

4. 10th York Coy. will leave ZILLEBEKE LAKE so as to arrive BUTTE de POLYGONE at about 3.30 p.m.

5. Completion of Relief will be reported by you to Brigade Headquarters at HOOGE CRATER.

6. Acknowledge.

Issued by runner
6 p.m. 26.10.17.

                                   V. F. Samuelson
                                                                         Captain,
                  & Adjutant   O X E N.

Appendix 20

Extract from Xth CORPS ROUTINE ORDER No.1826
dated 27th Oct. 1917.

1826. Under authority granted by His Majesty the King, the Corps Commander has awarded the following decorations to the undermentioned N.C.Os. and men for Gallantry in the Field on the dates stated:-

MILITARY MEDAL.

No.	Rank	Name	Regiment	Date
202312	Pte	C.J.Baker	R.W.Surrey Regt.	2.10.17.
205413	"	S.J.Blake	do.	4.10.17.
205471	" (L/C)	A.V.Lemon	do.	do.
206110	"	H.Homewood	do.	do.
205500	"	J. Capp	do.	7.10.17.
201126	Cpl	F.J.Linsey	do.	6.10.17.
201584	Pte (L/C)	C.C.Clark	do.	5.10.17.
205420	"	H.C.Dunkley	do.	4.10.17.
206844	" (L/C)	A.Shipp	do.	do.
200094	Sgt	W.T.C.Swarfield	do.	do.
205735	Pte	A. Dix	do.	2-7.10.17.
205499	"	B.W.Gallop	do.	4.10.17.
200770	Sgt	F. Reid	do.	do.
201348	"	A.V.Glaze	do.	do.

---oOo---

CONFIDENTIAL.

WAR DIARY

of the

3/4th BN "The "QUEEN'S" (R.W.S.) REGT

from

1st NOVEMBER, 1917 to 30th NOVEMBER, 1917

Army Form C. 2118.

WAR DIARY
or
INTELLIGENCE SUMMARY.
(Erase heading not required.)

Instructions regarding War Diaries and Intelligence Summaries are contained in F. S. Regs., Part II. and the Staff Manual respectively. Title pages will be prepared in manuscript.

Place	Date	Hour	Summary of Events and Information	Remarks and references to Appendices
CAMP "C" EAST of DICKEBUSCH.	NOVEMBER 1.		Strength of Battalion 31 officers 620 O.R. The Camp was improved by addition of extra tents & shelters.	MSS Appendix I
do.	2.		Training continued.	MSS
do.	3.		Brigade Relief. The battalion left camp at 3.30 p.m. & marched to the vicinity of the BUTTE de POLYGON where they went in support to 110th Brigade. Battalion Hd. with "A" Coy. marched to Clapham Junction on the MENIN ROAD where the 8th Leicestershire Regt. was relieved by 8.0 p.m. A quiet night. Casualties NIL.	MSS Appendix 2
do.	4.		Heavy shelling at dawn in retaliation to our barrages. At 7.0 p.m. the Company advance parties left to reconnoitre the front line. At 8.15 p.m. the half Battalion left CLAPHAM JUNCTION, to relieve the 6th Leicestershire Regiment on the front line around REUTEL RIDGE. B+D forming their positions in outpost to 'C' Coy on the centre & 'D' Coy on the right of the front line ie B+D was in close support. A quiet but very dark night. The 10th Yorkshire Regiment relieved the 62nd Brigade across on the left whilst the 1st Cheshire Regiment 15th Brigade still kept in line more in our rear ?.......? the 7th German division was opposite to us. Casualties killed 1 O.R. wounded 1 O.R.	MSS Appendix 2 Appendix 3 Appendix 4

(A7092). Wt. W12839/M1293. 75,000. 1/17. D. D. & L., Ltd. Forms/C.2118/14.

WAR DIARY or INTELLIGENCE SUMMARY
Army Form C. 2118.

Place	Date Nov 1917	Hour	Summary of Events and Information	Remarks and references to Appendices
Trenches around REUTEL	5.		At dawn the enemy heavily shelled our lines in retaliation to the Army Barrage. C Company especially in the trenches being severely bombarded. A quiet day. Patrols were sent out along our front during night but the enemy was not encountered. Pte Pte H. Bisoiwce from POLDERHOEK CHATEAU. Enemy seen moving round REUTEL CEMETRY during the day. Casualties 2nd Lt S.A. SHORTMAN wounded. NCR killed 13 O.R. wounded.	4:96 Appendix 3
do.	6.		The 5th Division attacked POLDERHOEK CHATEAU at 6am unsuccessfully. The enemy heavily shelled our front line in retaliation to our barrage. Kept up a steady bombardment of our back positions all the morning, and also scattered shooting on Battalion HQ, forcing them to move forward to the Company in support. Further hostile parties were seen moving in the vicinity of POLDERHOEK CHATEAU throughout the day. The enemy were not encountered by our patrols during the night. The O/C. 2nd 4/5 Yorks Company gassed met by 1 Sgt & 6 men was observed & were probably taken prisoner by the enemy. Casualties Lieut. PA. CURTOIS wounded. 2 O.R. killed 12 O.R. wounded 7 O.R. missing.	4:96 Appendix 3
do.	7.		The hostile retaliation to our Army Barrage at 3:10 a.m. being not so heavy as hitherto. A very quiet day. Further parties around POLDERHOEK CHATEAU were seen during the day. Track was gained with the 11th Yorkshire Regiment on our right & hostile M.G. was encountered in REUTEL CEMETRY Battalion HQ at the Company in support.	H:96 Appendix 3

WAR DIARY
INTELLIGENCE SUMMARY

Army Form C. 2118.

Place	Date	Hour	Summary of Events and Information	Remarks and references to Appendices
Trenches around REUTEL	7 Cont'd		were inspected by the Brigade & the BUTTE de POLYGON. Lt. Col. K.A. Oswald was awarded the D.S.O. & Capt. V.F. Danielson Hunt A.B. Scott were awarded the M.C. whilst 202962 Sgt. W. Nott was awarded the D.C.M. by the P.M.C. in C. Casualties by O.R. wounded	Appendix 5. M.C.C
do.	8		The usual bombardment of our lines by the enemy at dawn. Apparent day. Hostile aeroplanes were active above our sector during the morning. Major Estcourse & 1 Officer & 262 O.R. per Company arrived to reconnoitre the line preparatory to the relief by 12/13 Northumberland Fusiliers. The relief commenced at 8.0 p.m. but owing to the extreme darkness, it was not complete until 12 midnight. The hostile artillery was quiet. Casualties NIL	M.C.C Appendix 6
RAILWAY DUGOUTS ZILLIBEKE.	9		The Battalion were all present at 8.0 a.m. the night being so dark elements lost their way.	M.C.C
do.	10		Day spent in cleaning up.	M.C.C
do.	11		Relief by 1st Cheshire Reg't 15th Brigade 5th Division Battalion left 2.4/11/1932 at 2.30 p.m. arriving at No.13. MICMAC CAMP at 5.0 p.m. Divisional reserve. Ministerial both rachorodant thanks the groups, M.C	M.C.C Appendix 7
MIC MAC CAMP. West of DICKEBUSCH	12		Working party of 1 Officer & 50 O.R. for R.E. at ZILLIBEKE LAKE. The remainder of Battalion kept to baths.	M.C.C
do.	13		Day spent in inspections following up. 20175 Pte. ELLIS V.P. was awarded the Military Medal for work performed on Oct 4 1917. also 202364 Pte. LOVERING A.E.R. was awarded Military Medal whilst attached to Brigade as a Runner.	M.C.C Appendix 8

Army Form C. 2118.

WAR DIARY
or
INTELLIGENCE SUMMARY.
(Erase heading not required.)

Instructions regarding War Diaries and Intelligence Summaries are contained in F. S. Regs., Part II. and the Staff Manual respectively. Title pages will be prepared in manuscript.

Place	Date	Hour	Summary of Events and Information	Remarks and references to Appendices
MICMAC Camp W. of DICKEBUSCH	November 14		Training Commenced.	H.C.C
do.	15		Move to WESTOUTRE Area. The Battalion left MICMAC Camp at 8.30 a.m. & marched via LA CLYTTE & RENINGHELST to KENORA CAMP. N.E. of WESTOUTRE, arriving there at 11.30 a.m.	H.C.C Appendix 9
KENORA CAMP N.E. of WESTOUTRE	16		Training Continued.	H.C.C
do	17		The Division commenced its march to the 1st Army. 13th Corps Area. The battalion left Camp at 8.25 a.m. & marched via BAILLEUL & was billeted in farms south of OUTERSTEEN. Reaching its destination at 1.30 p.m.	H.C.C Appendix 10 Appendix 11
OUTERSTEEN	18		The Battalion left billets at 8.30 a.m. & marched via MERVILLE & HINGES to OBLINGHEM arriving at billets in the village at 4.0 p.m.	H.C.C Appendix 12
OBLINGHEM	19		The Battalion left billets at 8.25 a.m. marched via BETHUNE & HALLICOURT to BARLIN arriving in billets at 12.45 p.m.	H.C.C Appendix 13
BARLIN	20		The Battalion (less Transport which arranged) left billets at 9.40 a.m. marched via HERSIN VILLERS-AU-BOIS to the MOUNT ST ELOY Area where it was billeted in huts immediately at LE PENDU Camp, N.W. of MT. ST. ELOY arriving in billets at 2.0 p.m.	H.C.C Appendix 14
MOUNT ST. ELOY.	21		The Battalion left Camp at 8.15 a.m. marched via ANZIN to AUBREY CAMP on the LENS — ARRAS Road, South of ECURIE arriving at 12.15 p.m. MAJOR. E. A. SAWYER, D.S.O. Royal Berkshire Regiment took over the command of the Battalion.	H.C.C Appendix 15
AUBREY CAMP S. of ECURIE	22		Day spent in resting cleaning up. 2,3,5 & 8 Pk. WALK L.J. was awarded the Military Medal for work performed Oct 22 – 26th.	H.C.C Appendix 16

Army Form C. 2118.

WAR DIARY
or
INTELLIGENCE SUMMARY.
(Erase heading not required.)

Instructions regarding War Diaries and Intelligence Summaries are contained in F. S. Regs., Part II. and the Staff Manual respectively. Title pages will be prepared in manuscript.

Place	Date	Hour	Summary of Events and Information	Remarks and references to Appendices
AUBREY CAMP. S. of ÉCURIE.	NOVEMBER 23.		Working parties of 200 O.R. supplied to R.E. The back areas of the front line sys tem was reconnoitred by officers during the morning so that in the emergency of the enemy returning, our advanced operations at CAMBRAI, the battalion would be able to move forward	Appendix 17
do.	24.		without delay. Another working party of 200 O.R. supplied to R.E. Further officers M.Os reconnoitred the back areas of front line. A strength of 137 O.R. arrived more taken on the strength of the Battalion	No. C
do.	26.		Training commenced. Preparations were commenced to move the Division to another sector, all equipment &c being drawn up to requisitions & all officers & O.R. being asked to rejoin before the 30th inst. 2nd Lts. from courses	No. C Appendix 18.
do.	27.		Training continued. 2nd Lts. R.P. Riggs, J.A. Hunt, H.T. Sweet, G. Stevenson & T. Howells joined the Battalion for duty from the 1st Batt. "The Queen's" Regt.	No. C
do.	28.		Training continued	K.C.C
do.	29.		Training continued. 200098. Sgt. Phillips. B.E. was awarded the D.C.M. for work performed on Feb. 4. 1917.	No. C Appendix 19 No. C
do.	30.		Training continued. Orders were received to move during tomorrow to an area S.E. of enemy & attack South of CAMBRAI. The transport was bivouacked & marched by road, leaving AUBREY CAMP at 6.30 p.m. The battalion paraded at 11.45 p.m. to march to MAROEUIL for entraining purposes, a small portion of the transport had already started to march to MAROEUIL at 8.20 p.m. in order to accompany the Battalion	

Lt. Col. G. Hunt. Lt.
Commanding 1/4 Batt. "The Queens Regt."

Appendix 1.

3/4th Bn. "The Queen's" (R.W.S.) Regt.

Nominal Roll of Officers.

SUBSTANTIVE RANK.	ACTING RANK.	NAME.	Unit of Offrs. Att'd.
Captain	A/Major	H.C.Jannon, M.C.	1st Bn. "The Queen's"(RWS)Regt.
Captain		A.S.Ashby	2/5th Bn. do. do.
Captain		A.E.Harper	
Captain		F.G.Tait	
Lieut.	A/Captain	A.T.Latham	
Lieut.	A/Captain	V.E.Samuelson	
Lieut.	A/Capt.& Adjutant	E.W.Preston	
Lieut.	A/Captain	L.I.S.Vidler	
Lieut.		R.E.Sparkes	
Lieut.	A/Captain	E.A.Forides	
Lieut.		W.P.McCabe	
Lieut.		K.T.Carter	
Lieut.		.S.Frost	
Lieut.		F.R.A.Mackall	
Lieut.		F.A.Curtois	2/6th Bn. Suffolk Regt.
Lieut.		R.A.D.Bannerman	
Lieut.		A.J.Jenn	
Lieut.		G.F.Cockburn	do.
Lieut.		H.W.Flax	
Lieut.		G.J.Thomas	1st City of London Regt.
Lieut.		H.J.Eason	2/6th Suffolk Regt.
Lieut.		J.W.Skeet	2nd City of London Regt.
2/Lt.		H.G.Gilliland, M.C.	1st Devon Regt.
2/Lt.		N.E.Paterson	19th North'ld. Fusiliers.
2/Lt.		L. Hall	3rd do. do.
2/Lt.		C.Tayler	1st & 2nd B."The Queen's"
2/Lt.		F.Wallace	do. (RWS)Regt.
2/Lt.		J.R.Sheppard	do.
2/Lt.		H.J.Trotman	do.
2/Lt.		A.T.Calvert	"The Queen's"(RWS)Regt.
2/Lt.		T.L.Birch	
Hon.Lieut.& Q.M.			
Captain & Rev. (C.F.)		M.Iron, D.S.O., M.C.	attached.
Lieut.		M. O'Reilly, R.A.M.C.	attached.

Major.
Commanding 3/4th Bn."The Queen's"(RWS)Regt.

31.10.17.

Appendix 2

OPERATION ORDER No. 12   Copy No. 10
by Major H.S.Cannon, M.C.
Commanding Q.E.R.R.

Ref.Map Sheet 28
BECH FARM.   3rd November, 1917.

1. The 62nd Inf.Brigade will relieve the 110th Inf.Brigade between 3rd and 5th November, in the right sector of the Division front.

2. The 3/4th "Queen's" (R.W.S.)Regt. will relieve the 7th Leicestershire Regt. in support tonight. "B" and "D" Coys. being in the vicinity of BUTTE de POLYGON, when Capt. A.T.DeTHAM will be in command of the half Battalion.
    "A" and "C" Coys. & Battn.H.Q.Coy. at CLAPHAM JUNCTION.

3. The Battalion will leave its present camp in the following order, at 3.30 p.m. sharp:-
    "B" Coy. - "D" Coy. - Bn.H.Q's.Coy. - "C" Coy. - "A" Coy. meeting guides at the rate of 2 per Company at HOOGE CRATER at 5.30 p.m. Movement West of ZILLEBEKE by Companies 250 yards interval, East of ZILLEBEKE by platoons 100 yards interval.

4. O.Cs. "B" and "D" Companies will report "relief complete" to CLAPHAM JUNCTION by Codeword "L A R K E R".

5. Blankets will be rolled (in tens) clearly labelled and taken to Q.M. stores by 10.0 a.m. Packs, greatcoats and Officers' kits will be stacked in Transport Lines by 2.0 p.m.
    The Battalion will parade at 3.15 p.m. Dress:- Fighting order, leather jerkins to be worn.

6. Two days' rations will be carried on the men in addition to Iron rations, and all ranks must carry one pair of clean socks.

7. Four Lewis Gun Limbers and one Limber for H.Q's. Coy. will accompany their respective Coys. with Lewis Guns, Magazines, Rations and Officers' Trench kits to Junction of track in MENIN ROAD, East of HOOGE CRATER reporting at Camp "C" at 2 p.m.

8. O.C.Companies will each send 1 Officer, 1 N.C.O. and 2 runners on the morning of November 4th to report at Battalion H.Q's. 6th Leicester Regt. J.10.c.Central, to reconnoitre the front line. Time to be notified later.

9. The Battalion will relieve the 6th Leicester Regt. in the front line on the night of 4/5th November. Guides for "B" and "D" Coys. will be at BUTTE de POLYGON at 6.0 p.m. and guides for remainder of Battalion at CLAPHAM JUNCTION at 8.15 p.m.

10. Dispositions of the Battalion in the front line will be :-
    "D" Coy. on right - "C" Coy.Centre - "B" Coy. Left, "A" Co.Support.

11. Relief will be reported complete to Bn.H.Q's. J.10.c.Central by Codeword "I G N I T E".

12. Carrying party will be the same as last, namely, 1 N.C.O. and 9 men per Company, under Lieut. S.J.Mason. Further instructions will be issued. Packs will be carried - Blankets dumped at Q.M.Stores.

13. All ranks detailed as Nucleus Party will report to Lieut.Carter at present Bn.H.Q's. at 4 p.m. and proceed to Divisional Detail Camp. under Senior C.S.M. Unconsumed portion of day's rations will be carried. Packs and blankets will be carried. Each Coy. will have a nominal roll ready to be handed to Lieut.Carter by Senior N.C.O.

14. All lines will be left thoroughly clean.

15. Acknowledge.

(signature)

Captain & Adjutant,
3/4th Bn. "The Queen's" (R.W.S.) Regt.

Issued by Orderly Sergts: at 9.30 a.m.

Copy No. 1 Filed.
" " 2-6 Coy.Commanderd & H.Q.Coy.
" " 7 Q.M.& T.O.
" " 8 32nd Inf.Bde.
" " 9/10 War Diary.

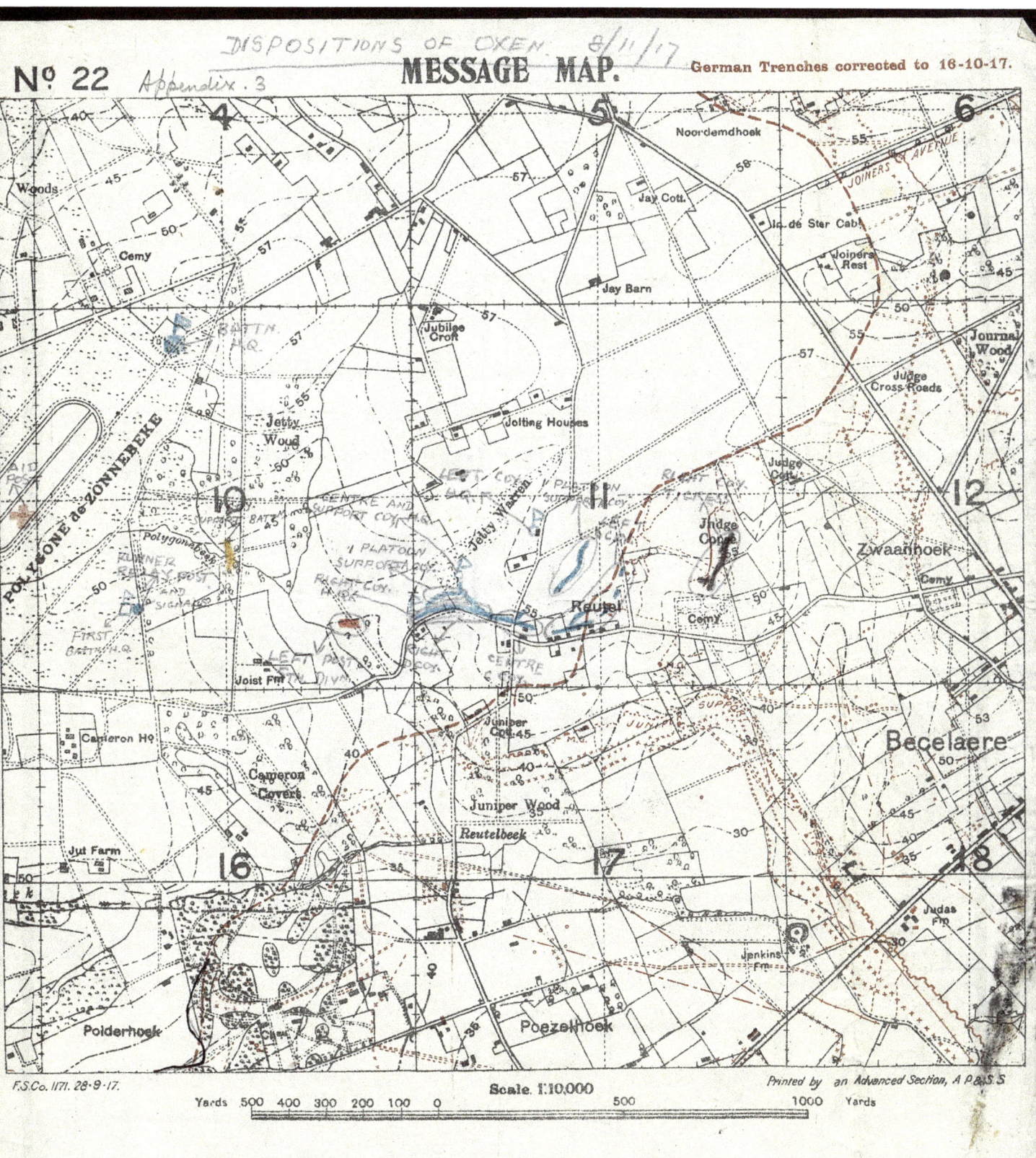

Appendix 4

DEFENCE SCHEME FOR
O X E N.
Right Battalion, Right Sector (REUTEL).

Copy No. 8

1. The front line will be held at all costs.

2. In the event of the left of the line being captured by the enemy, the platoon in support at J.11.c.8.6 will counterattack immediately over the open.

3. In the event of the enemy penetrating the right of the line, the platoon in support at J.11.c.2.5 will make an immediate counter-attack over the open, also sending a bombing squad along trench at J.11.c.15.45, whilst the centre Company will bomb along the trench towards the right.

4. In the event of a hostile attack succeeding in the centre of the line, both the platoons in support will make an immediate counter-attack over the open covered by Lewis Gun fire from both flank Companies. O.C. "D" Coy. will also bomb along the trench from the right.

5. The Company of BEAR in support at J.10.c.9.5 will hold themselves in readiness to move, and will await orders from O.C. OXEN, upon receipt of which they will move forward and occupy the line of the track through J.11.c.60.45, with a defensive flank facing South.

6. In the event of the enemy penetrating the lines of the Battalions on the flanks, the 2 platoons in support will form defensive flanks; on the left through Coy. H.qs. at J.11.c.6.8 facing North; on the right they will move sufficiently far forward from their present line to obtain a good field of fire towards CAMERON HOUSE. The Company in support will hold themselves in readiness to move, and await orders from O.C. OXEN.

Battalion H.Q. are situated at J.10.c.50.45.

The Regimental Aid Post is situated at J.9.d.9.9.

H.C. Cameron Major,
Commanding O X E N.

5.11.17.

Copies to -
Nos. 1-4 Companies.
" 5 Support Company BEAR.
" 6 TIGRESS.
" 7 BOLT.
" 8-9 War Diary.

Copy.

Appendix. S.

BRIGADE ORDERS

by

Brigadier-General G.H.GATER, D.S.O., Commanding

62nd Infantry Brigade.

6th Novr., 1917.

3. Under authority granted by His Majesty the King, the Field Marshall Commanding-in-Chief has awarded the following decorations to the undermentioned Officers and other ranks for gallantry in the Field on the dates stated:-

The Distinguished Service Order

Major (a/Lt.Col.) K.A.Oswald,	R.W.Surrey Regt.	4.10.17.

Bar to the Military Cross

Capt. C. Jacobs, M.C.	R.A.M.C., att. Lincoln Regt.	4.10.17.

The Military Cross

Lt. (A/Capt.) V.F.Samuelson	R.W.Surrey Regt.	5.10.17.
2/Lt. (a/Lt.) A.B.Frost	do.	4.10.17.
T/Lt. J.McKinnon	Northd. Fus.	4.10.17.
T/2/Lt. C.N.Edmonds	do.	do.
T/2/Lt. W.S.Hutchinson	do.	do.
2/Lt. S.B.Edinborough	Lincoln Regt.	do.
2/Lt. F.H.Young	do.	do.
Lieut. H.W.Clarke	Lincoln Regt. att. M.Gun Corps	do.
T/2/Lt. T.A.Hyslop	Yorkshire Regt.	do.
Rev. J.T.Tunstall	Army Chaplains' Dept. attached Lincolns Regt.	4-5.10.17.

Bar to the Distinguished Conduct Medal.

11348. C.S.M. W.H.Scott	Northd. Fus.	4.10.17.

The Distinguished Conduct Medal.

9497 C.S.M. G.W.Wood	Lincolns Regt.	4.10.17.
202962 Sgt. W. Mort	R.W.Surrey Regt.	do.
9343 C.Q.M.S. W.S.Senior	Northd. Fus.	do.
24246 Sgt. J.D.Jefferson	do.	do.
9388 L/Cpl. H.Bombrose	Lincolns Regt.	do.
9827 Pte F. Matthews	do.	do.
4936 C.S.M. H.F.Calletly	M.G.Corps.	4-5.10.17.

(Sgd.) C.O.P. Gibson,

Captain
Staff Captain
62nd Infantry Brigade.

Appendix 6

OPERATION ORDER No. 19   Copy No. 9
by Major H.C.CANNON, M.C.,
Commanding O X E N.

Map Ref:
BECELEARE.   7.11.17.

1. The Batt. will be relieved by BEAR in front Line on the night of the 8/9th Nov.

2. Disposition: BEAR will take over front line with two Coys. only, namely,
"C" Coy. BEAR will take over from "D" Coy. and right half of "C" Coy. OXEN.
"B" Coy. BEAR will take over from "B" Coy. and left half of "C" Coy. OXEN.
"D" Coy. BEAR will relieve "A" Coy. OXEN.

3. Guides will be furnished as follows:-
Two guides from "B" Coy. and one from "C" Coy. will report to O.C. "B" BEAR at MEBU just vacated by Bn.H.Qs. tonight at 4 p.m.
Two guides from "D" Coy. and one from "C" Coy. will report O.C. "C" Coy. BEAR, BUTTE de POLYGONE at 4 p.m.
Two guides from "A" Coy. will report O.C. "D" Coy. BEAR at the BUTT de POLYGONNE at 6 p.m.

4. On completion of relief O.C. Companies will hand in relief complete by code word "TRON" to Sergt. HARDING at Signal Office, old Bn.H.Qs. at J.10.c.central. Coys. will then proceed to RAILWAY DUGOUTS where guides will meet them at Archway where light railway passes through embankment.
H.Qs. Coy. on receipt of relief complete from the four Coys. and having handed over Signals to BEAR, Sergt. HARDING will send the Codeword through to Bn.H.Qs. which will mean all 4 Coys. have been relieved.

5. All grenades, rifle grenades, S.O.S. Signals, Lewis Gun Magazines, maps, etc. will be handed over on relief.

6. O.C.Companies are reminded that 1" Very Pistols and Vigilant Periscopes are not Trench Stores, and will not be handed over.

7. Acknowledge.

V.Samuelson
Capt. & Adjutant
O X E N.

Issued by Runner at 4 a.m.
Copy No. 1 Filed.
"   "   2-6 Coys.& H.Q.Coy.
"   "   7 BOLT.
"   "   8 BEAR.
"   "   9-10 War Diary.

Appendix 7

OPERATION ORDER No. 20
by Major H.C.CANNON, M.C.
Commanding O X E N.

Copy No. 9

Ref: Sheet 28.   11.11.17.

1. The 62nd Inf. Bde. will be relieved by the 15th Inf. Bde. between 11th and 14th Nov.

2. This Battalion will be relieved by the 1st Cheshire Regt. to-day at 2.30 p.m.

3. The Battalion will move by route march to No. 13 MicMac Camp, leaving as under :-
"A" Coy. 2.32 p.m. - "B" Coy. 2.35 p.m. - "C" Coy. 2.39 p.m. - "D" Coy. 2.43 p.m. - Bn. H.Qs. will move at 2.30 p.m.
Interval 100 yds. between Coys. March by Companies.

4. Route - SHRAPNEL CORNER - KRUISSTRAATEHOEK - CAFE BELGÉ - DICKEBUSCH - HALLEBAST.
A guide will meet each Coy. at HALLEBAST CORNER to conduct to Camp.

5. Teas will be issued on arrival.

6. All Huts etc. must be left clean.

7. Acknowledge.

                                            VJHamilton M.C.
                                            Capt. & Adjutant,
                                            O X E N.

Issued by runner at 12.15.
Copy No. 1 Filed.
  "   " 2-6 Coys.
  "   "   7 BOLT.
  "   " 8-9 War Diary.

EXTRACT FROM :- Appendix 8

Xth CORPS ROUTINE ORDERS

BY

Lieut-General Sir T. L. N. Morland, K.C.B., K.C.M.G., D.S.O.

November 12th, 1917.

ADJUTANT GENERAL'S BRANCH.

1924. IMMEDIATE AWARDS.

Under authority granted by His Majesty the King, the Corps Commander has awarded the following Decorations to the undermentioned N.C.O's and men for gallantry in the Field on the dates stated :-

The MILITARY MEDAL.

| No 201175, Pte V. F. Ellis. | R. W. S. Regt | 5. 10. 17. |
| ,, 202364, Pte G.E.R. Lovering. | R. W. S. Regt. att R. E. | 20. 10. 17 |

Appendix 9

OPERATION ORDER No.21   Copy No. 9
by Major H.C.CANNON,M.C.
Commanding 3 & 4 B.N.

Ref. Sheet 28.   13.11.17.

1. The 62nd Inf. Bde. will move from No. 4 Area to WESTOUTRE on Nov 15th by route march.

2. The Battalion will move from present camp in following order at 8.30 a.m. on the 15th inst.
    Bn H. Q. Coy,   "B",   "C",   "D",   "A" Coys –Transport Section.
    The following distances will be observed on line of march.
            Between Battalions   500 yards.
            ,,   Companies   100 ,,
            ,,   Units & l's
            ,,   Transport   100 ,,

3. The strictest march discipline will be maintained on the march.

4. Route: Road Junction N.32.d.8.1 - Cross Roads N.3.c.4.2 - LA CLYTTE Road Junction M.17.c.5.5 - WESTOUTRE - Camp KENORA N.3.c.9.7.

5. Each Coy Commander will detail 1 N. C. O to report to Lieut N. B. Sparkes at Bn Headquarters tomorrow, 14th inst at 8. 30 a.m. to proceed and take over camp and remain; reporting to Staff Captain, 62nd Infantry Brigade at Area Commandant, WESTOUTRE, at 10 a.m. Officer's kit will be left at Q. M. Stores by 8. a.m. and be conveyed over to camp.

6. All officers' kits to be at Q. M's Stores by 7. 30 a.m. 15th inst. Blankets rolled in tens and labelled by Co's to be at Q. M's Stores by 7 a.m. 15th inst.
    Lewis Gun Limbers will be loaded under Coy's arrangements by 4 p.m. 14th inst.
    Coy Officers' Canteens must be loaded on Coy Lewis Gun Limbers by 7. 30 a.m. 15th inst.
    On the 15th inst, breakfasts will be served at 6 a.m.; dinners will be cooked on route and served on arrival in camp.

7. All lines must be left thoroughly clean and a certificate sent Headquarters by 8 a.m. to this effect.

8. Acknowledge.

                                        Captain & Adjutant.
                                        3/4th Bn "The Queen's" (R.W.S.)Regt.

Issued by Orderly at 7.0 p.m.,
        13th inst.
Copy No 1. Filed.
    ,, ,, 2-6 Coy Commanders.
    ,, ,, 7. 62nd Inf Bde.
    ,, ,, 8. Q. M. & T. O.
    ,, ,, 9-10 War Diary.

Appendix 10

CONFIDENTIAL.

G. O. C. and all Ranks,
    21st Division.

    On your departure from Xth Corps I wish to thank you for all your good and gallant work whilst under my command.

    In parting from you, which I do with regret I wish you all good luck in the future.

                                   T. L. N. Morland,
                                        Lieut-General,
                          Commanding Xth Corps.

17th November, 1917.

Appendix II

OPERATION ORDER No. 22 Copy No. 9
by Major H.C.GANNON, M.C.,
Commanding 3/4th Bn. "The Queen's" (RWS) Regt.

Ref. Sheet
HAZEBROUCK 5a. Sheet 28.   16.11.17.

1. The 21st Division is being transferred from the 2nd Army to the 1st Army by route march. On arrival in 1st Army Area the 21st Division will join XIII Corps.

2. The 62nd Inf. Brigade will move on the 17th, the Battalion moving as under from its present Quarters, leaving at 8.25 a.m:-

   Bn.H.Qs. - "C" Co. - "D" Co. - "A" Co. - "B" Co. - Transport Section.

3. Route:- WESTOUTRE - LOCRE - BAILLEUL - OULTERSTEENE.
   Throughout march the greatest attention will be paid to march discipline -
   (a) All Coys. will halt 10 minutes before each clock hour and will resume the march at the clock hour.
   (b) The following distances will be maintained between Coys. on the march:-
       Coys. 100 yds. - Unit & Transport Section 100 yds.

4. Midday meal will be cooked en route, and served immediately on arrival.
   Officers' Valises will be at Q.M.Stores by 7.30 a.m.
   Blankets rolled and labelled, in tens, Q.M.Stores by 7 a.m.
   Sick parade 7.30 a.m.
   Coy.Officers' Canteens on L.G.Limbers by 7.45 a.m.
   Breakfasts will be served at 6.30 a.m.

5. Guides from Billeting parties will meet Coys. at Cross Roads S. of O in OULTERSTEENE to guide to billets.

6. All lines must be left thoroughly clean.

7. Acknowledge.

                                           Captain & Adjutant,
                                    3/4th Bn. "The Queen's" (R.W.S.) Regt.

Issued by Runner at 3.0 p.m.
16.11.17.
Copy No. 1 Filed.
  "   " 2-6 Coy.Commanders & H.Q.Coy.
  "   " 7 62nd Inf. Bde.
  "   " 8 T.O.& Q.M.
  "   " 9-10 War Diary.

Appendix 12

Copy No. 9.

OPERATION ORDER No. 23 by
Major H. C. Cannon, M.C.,
Commanding 3/4th. Bn. "The Queen's" (RWS) Regt.

Ref. Sheet HAZEBROUCK 5a.   17/11/17.

No. 1. The 62nd. Inf. Bde. will continue to march into 1st Army Area tomorrow 18th inst. The Battalion will rendez-vous at road junction due EAST of M in METEREN (Blue River) at 8.30 a.m. in following order.
Battalion H.Q. - "C" Coy - Transport Section facing West - "D" Coy - A Coy - B Coy facing south.

No. 2. Same intervals and march dicipline as to-day.

No. 3. Route - NEUFBERQUIN - MERVILLE - ROBECQ - to Billet area.

No. 4. All Blankets to be returned QM. Stores by 7.30 a.m.
Coy. Cookers and L.G. Limbers will accompany Coys. to rendez-vous and await instructions.
Horses for above will be at Coy. H.Q. at 8.10 a.m. sharp.
Sick Parade at 7.30 a.m. and men must parade in full marching Order.

No. 5. Acknowledge.

Issued by Orderly Sergeants at 7 p.m.

Copy No. 1.   Filed.
       2-6   Coy. Commanders.
       7.   T.O. & Q.M.
       8.   62nd. Inf. Bde.
       9-10   War Diary.

V. F. Sammulon.
Captain & Adjutant.
OXEN.

Appendix. 13

OPERATION ORDER No. 24 by
Major H.C. Cannon, M.C.
OXEN.

Copy No. 10.

Ref. HAZEBROUCK 5a.
LENS II.

18/11/17.

No. 1.   The Battalion will continue march 19th inst to HAILLICOURT.

Rendez-vous at 8.25 a.m. in following order with Battalion H.Q. Company's head where railway crosses main road of this village. Battalion H.Q. - "A" - "B" - Band - "C" - "D" Coys.,-Transport Section.

No. 2.   Blankets - Officers' Valises to be at Q.M. Stores by 7.30 a.m. sharp.

Coys' Cookers and L.G. Limbers will rejoin Transport Section on the way to Rendez-vous.

Horses to be at respective Coys' H.Q. by 8.5 a.m.

Sick Parade at 7.30 a.m. - Dress Battle Order.

Mens' Packs will be carried by Lorries same as to-day.

Midday meal will be cooked on route.

Issued by Orderly Sergeants 7 p.m. 18/11/17.

Copy No. 1.   Filed.
     2-6   Coys.
     7.   Q.M.
     8.   T.O.
     9.   62nd Bde.
     10-11. War Diary.

Captain & Adjutant.
OXEN.

Appendix 14   Copy No. 10.

OPERATION ORDER No. 25 by
Major M. C. CANNON, M.C.,
Commanding 3/4th Bn. "The Queen's" (RWS) Regt.

Map Ref. LENS, II.   19th November, 1917.

No. 1.   The battalion will continue to march tomorrow, 20th inst., and will rendez-vous at 9.40 a.m., at level crossing due south of B in BAILIN.

Following order Battalion Headquarters - "B" - "C" - Band - "D" - "A" Companies.

No. 2.   Destination MT. ELOY area.

No. 3.   Blankets - Packs - Officers' Valises to be at QM. Stores by 8 a.m. sharp.

Horses for L.G. Limbers and Cookers to be at Coys' H.Q. by 8 a.m. and proceed direct to Transport lines.

Sick Parade at 8 a.m. Town Major's Office.

Packs will be carried by Lorries.

Midday Meal will be served on arrival at destination.

No. 4.   Acknowledge.

Issued by Orderly Sergeants at   p.m. 19/11/17.

Copy No. 1.   Filed.
        2-6.   Coys' Commanders.
        7.   Transport Officer.
        8.   Quartermaster.
        9.   62nd Bde.
        10-11. War Diary.

                                V. F. Parmenton
                                Captain & Adjutant.
                                OXEN.

Appendix. 15

Copy No. 10.

OPERATION ORDER No. 26
by Major H. C. CANNON, M.C.

Sheet 51B.
Map Ref. LENS 11.   20/11/17.

No. 1.   The Battalion will move by route march from

LE PENDU CAMP tomorrow 21st inst, to AUBREY CAMP (G.4.a.2.7.),

parading on Battalion Parade Ground ready to move at 8.45 a.m.

in following order :-

Bn. H.Q. Coy - "C" - "D" - Band - "A" - "B" Coys., Transport

Section.

No. 2.   Route :- MONT ST. ELOY - ANZIN - left handed to Ecurie Camp.

No. 3.   Blankets - Packs - Officers' Valises to be at Q. M. Stores by

8 a.m.   Sick Parade 7.30 a.m.

Midday meal will be cooked on route and served on arrival.

No. 4. Acknowledge.

Issued by Orderly Sergeants 11 p.m. 20/11/17.

Copy No. 1.   Filed.
        2-6.   Coy. Commanders.
        7.   Transport Officer.
        8.   Quartermaster.
        9.   62nd. Bde.
        10 & 11.   War Diary.

                                                   Captain & Adjutant.
                                                3/4 Bn "The Queens" R W S Rgt

Appendix 16

BRIGADE ORDERS

by

Brigadier-General G. H. Gater, D.S.O., Commanding

62nd Infantry Brigade.

---

8. <u>Honours and Rewards</u>.

The following N. C. O's and men have been awarded the Military Medal :-

<u>12/13 Northd Fus</u>.

10560	Sgt S.	Carr.
17578	Pte J. P.	Turner.
15329	" T.	Gair.
27764	" T.	Tuck.

<u>3/4 "Queen's" Regt</u>.

205039   Pte L. J. Wall.

<u>1 Lincolns Regt</u>.

8000   Cpl T. Cushley

<u>10 Yorks Regt</u>.

19541	Pte S. M.	Bowden.
33100	" A. E.	Green.
15836	Cpl G.	Snaith.

G.O.P. Gibson, Captain.
Staff Captain
62nd Infantry Brigade.

22nd Novr, 1917.

SECRET. 3/4th Bn "QUEEN's" (RWS) REGT. COPY NO. 12.

INSTRUCTIONS. - NO 1.

Ref: Map.
FOOT HILL. Sheet 1/20000.

24th NOV/17.

1. If the operations in progress on the Third Army Front attain further success, it is possible that the enemy may withdraw opposite the XIII Corps Front.

2. The task of the 62nd Brigade, in conjunction with the 64th Brigade will be either :-

   (a) To support the advance of the 31st Division, or
   (b) If required to push forward through the 31st Division and carry on the advance, or
   (c) To be prepared to hold our present trench system in case of necessity.

3. On receipt of orders to move, the Battalion acting in support to the remainder of the Brigade, will move to the Red Line North of GAVRELLE/to BAILLEUL ROAD.
   Road

4. The Red Line will be occupied in the following order from right to left - "A" - "B" - "C" - Hd Qrs Coy - "D" Coy.

5. Coys will move off in the above order and will march via ECOLINCOURT - ARRAS - BAILLEUL ROAD - to railway junction about M.1.b.5.5. - thence direct to their positions in Red Line.

6. All Officers & a proportion of N. C. O's and runners will reconnoitre the ground over which they will have to move, special attention being paid to -
   (a) Roads & tracks leading towards Front Line.
   (b) Communication trenches.
   (c) Positions either in trenches or behind cover where troops can be most conveniently assembled.
   (d) Dumps - Water Points - Regtl Aid Posts.

7. The Regtl Aid Post will be established in DITCH POST.

8. Bn Hd Qrs will be in dug-out at present occupied by right Coy. Hd Qrs now in Red Line.

9. Special Orders will be issued as regards movement of Transport Section & Q. M. Stores.

10. Acknowledge.

Captain & Adjutant,
3/4th Bn "The Queen's" (RWS) Regt.

Issued by Orderly Sergeants.

Copy No 1 Filed.
    "   2 - 6 Coy Comdrs - H.Q.Coy
    "   7 Transport Officer.
    "   8. Quartermaster.
    "   9. 62nd Infantry Bde.
    "   10. M. O.
    "   11. Commanding Officer.
    "   12-13. War Diary

COPY.

Appendix 18

Dear Cannon,

Now that you are about to have time to refit and reorganise, I hope you will give the most careful attention to the way your men turn out and salute.

Owing to drafts, etc., there was a considerable falling off, in the latter respect/at any rate, throughout the Division towards the end of the summer. If any men in this world have reason to be proud of themselves it is the men of this Division, and they can show their pride by the smartness of their turn out and in saluting.

Good turn out and good saluting are the Hall Marks of a good Division. I hope you will impress this on all ranks.

To obtain good results you must ensure the cooperation of all your officers and N.C.O.s. which I know they will cheerfully give if they realise how important these matters are.

My very best congratulations to you and to the Battalion on the magnificent work you have all done under the most trying comditions. I hope shortly to have the chance of conveying my congratulations to the Battalion in person.

Yours sincerely,

(Sd) David M. Campbell.

H.Q. 21st Division
19th Nov, 1917.

Appendix 19

EXTRACT FROM REGIMENTAL ORDERS, DATED 29th NOV/17.

NO 1493,- AWARDS.

Under authority granted by His Majesty the King, the Field Marshall Commanding in Chief has awarded the following decoration to the undermentioned N. C. O for Gallantry in the Field on the date stated, viz the Distinguished Conduct Medal :-

No 200088, Sergt Phillips, R.E.   4/10/17.

(Authority Xth Corps M.S./36 D/28/11/17.

Army Form C. 2118.

WAR DIARY
or
INTELLIGENCE SUMMARY.
(Erase heading not required.)

Instructions regarding War Diaries and Intelligence Summaries are contained in F.S. Regs., Part II. and the Staff Manual respectively. Title pages will be prepared in manuscript.

Place	Date	Hour	Summary of Events and Information	Remarks and references to Appendices
HEUDECOURT.	DECEMBER 22.		Training Continued	K.C.C
do.	24.		Training Continued. The C.O. & O.C. "A" Coy. recommended hereto preparatory to relief.	K.C.C
do.	25.		Dinner for men at 1.0 p.m. & for Sergeants during evening. Rainy snowy. 2016533 Sgt. FOG W.S. awarded Military Medal for work performed on December 1st 1917.	K.C.C Appendix 1
do.	26.		Transport & D.H.I. lines moved to VILLERS FAUCON whilst 62nd Brigade relieved 64th Brigade in front-line. the Batt'n relieving 9th. K.O.Y.L.I. regiment, the relief being complete by 6.30 p.m. "A" Coy. was on right "B" Coy. in left in front line whilst "C" Coy. was on right "D" Coy. on left in support. Hostile artillery slightly active around Batt'n H.Q. Casualties 2. O.R. Wounded.	K.C.C Appendix 2 do. 3 do. 9
Trenches around VAUCELETTE FARM & GLOUZEAUCOURT.	27.		BIRCHWOOD COPSE was included in the Battalion front. Very quiet day & night. Active protective patrolling throughout hours of dark. Casualties NIL.	K.C.
do.	28.		Again extremely quiet. A patrol recommended the front, no signs of enemy was encountered. Inter Company relief. "C" Coy. relieving "A" Coy. "D" Coy. relieving "B" Coy. Casualties NIL.	K.C.C
do.	29.		Day & night both very quiet.	K.C.C

Army Form C. 2118.

WAR DIARY
or
INTELLIGENCE SUMMARY.
(Erase heading not required.)

Instructions regarding War Diaries and Intelligence Summaries are contained in F.S. Regs., Part II. and the Staff Manual respectively. Title pages will be prepared in manuscript.

Place	Date	Hour	Summary of Events and Information	Remarks and references to Appendices
Trenches around VAUCELETTE FARM S. of GOUZEAUCOURT	DECEMBER 30.		Hostile artillery slightly active. "C"Coy's front support lines intermittently shelled. Orders received that Brigade front will be held by only 2 Batt's after 31st inst. Casualties Wounded 3 O.R. A draft. of 92 O.R. joined Batt'n.	H.C.C. Appendix 2.
do.	31.		Quiet day. Hit hostile artillery active in vicinity of Batt'n H.Q. during the evening. The Batt'n was relieved by 1st Lincolns & 13th Northumberland Fus. Regts in accordance with plan mentioned on 30th inst. The relief was complete by 6.0 p.m. The Batt'n moved to HEUDECOURT & was accommodated in huts to N.W. of Village. The transport + Q.M. Stores moved from VILLARS FAUCON. Casualties Nil.	H.C.C. Appendix 9. do. 2.

G. Heron
Lieut. Col.
Commanding 3/4 Batt'n "The Queen's" Reg't

Appendix 1

OPERATION ORDER NO 29

Copy No. 12

By Lt Col G. H. Sawyer, D. S. O., Commanding

3/4th Bn "The Queen's" (RWS) Regt.

SECRET.   8.12.17

Ref Sheet 57 c S. E.

1. The 62nd Infantry Bde will relieve the 64th Infantry Bde in the Left Sector of the Div Front on the 9th/10th December.

2. This Battalion will relieve the 1st E. Yorks Regt in the centre Sub Sector.

3. The Battalion will parade on the Battalion Parade ground ready to move off at 1.30 p.m.   Formation Mass.
Coys of this Battalion will relieve corresponding Coys of the 1st East Yorks Regt.

4. All Grenades, Rifle Grenades, S. A. A., S. O. S Signals, Maps, Defence Schemes etc will be taken over on relief.

5. Completion of Relief will be reported to Bn H. Q's by Code Word - "BARRE"

6. Administrative Orders will be issued separately.

7. Guides from 1st E. Yorks Regt, 2 per Coy and 1 Bn H. Q's Coy will meet Battalion at level crossing W 16 c 0 7 at 5 p.m.

8. Advance Party, consisting as under, will report to a guide 1st E. Yorks Regt at 10 a.m. at HEUDICOURT W.21.a.6.8..

   Each Coy   1 Officer - 1 N.C.O - 1 L.G.N.C.O - 2 Signallers.

   H. Q's Coy 1 Officer - Sergt Hunt - 2 Signallers,
              Sergt Lancaster - 2 Pioneers.

9. Acknowledge.

Issued by Runner 4 p.m., 8/12/17.

Copy No 1   Filed.
     ,,   2 - 6   Coy Commanders & H.Q's Coy.
     ,,   7   62nd Inf Bde.
     ,,   8   Q. M.
     ,,   9   T. O.
     ,,   10   1st E. Yorks Regt.
     ,,   11 & 12 War Diary.

Captain & Adjutant,
3/4th Bn "The Queen's" (RWS) Regt.

Appendix 3

DEFENCE SCHEME, 3/4th "Queen's"   Secret.

1. The Bn holds the centre sub-sector of the Brigade Front.

   Right Bn Boundary   -   LEITH WALK exclusive X.13.c.9.0.
   Left Bn Boundary   -   about X.13.c.8.6.

2. DISTRIBUTION - FRONT LINE -
   "A" Coy on right, "B" Coy on left - each Coy has 4 Lewis Guns in front line & 2 Sections in support.
   "C" Coy is in support to front held by "A" Coy & "D" Coy in support to "B" Coy.

   A Coy of the Pioneer Bn & the Hd Q's Coy plus a Lewis Gun Section from C & D Coys will form the garrison of the Strong Point - W.18.d.8.1.

   4 Trench Mortars cover VAUCELLETTE FARM.

3. ACTION IN CASE OF ATTACK. (i) All troops will immediately stand to.
   (ii) The front line is the main line of resistance & must be held at all costs.
   (iii) Should the enemy gain a footing in the front line he will be immediately counter attacked by supports in the hands of O.C. Coys. Should this fail to dislodge him, a counter attack will be ordered by C or D Coys or both.
   (iv) Should the Farm be captured, a counter attack will be made by order of the Comdg Officer by "C" Coy attacking from the South and "D" Coy from the West, supported by fire from Trench Mortars.
   (v) Any working parties from other units which may be in the Bn Area will at once come under the command of the nearest O.C. Coy.

4. The S.O.S. Signal is a rifle grenade bursting into two green & two white stars.

5. Acknowledge.

   1 Copy issued to each Coy Commander by Runner at 11 a.m., 10/12/17.

                                           Lt-Colonel,
                              Commanding 3/4th Bn "The Queen's"(R.W.S.) Regt.

10.12.17.

Appendix 4   Secret

OPERATION ORDER NO 30.

BY LT. COL. G.H. SAWYER, D.S.O. COMMANDING "OXEN".

Copy No. 9.
12-12-17.

1. The two companies in support will relieve the two companies in front line today.
   "C" Coy. relieving "A" Coy.
   "D" Coy. relieving "B" Coy.
2. Coy. Commanders will be notified hour of relief to commence from this Office later. It will not commence before dinner hour.
3. All details regarding relief will be made direct between Company Commanders concerned.
4. All Grenades - Rifle Grenades - S.A.A. - Signals - Maps - Defence Schemes, etc., will be taken over on relief.
5. Completion of relief by will be notified to Bn. H.Q's by code word - HIGGS
6. Guards now furnished O.C. "D" Coy. will be relieved by "C" Coy. on completion of relief when the "D" Coy. men will rejoin their Coy. in front line.

Issued by Runner.
9 a.m. 12/12/17.

(Signed) V. F. Samuelson,
Captain & Adjutant,
OXEN.

Secret.

OPERATION ORDER NO. 30, BY

Appendix 5

LT. COL. G. H. SAWYER D.S.O., COMMANDING OXEN.

Map Reference 57cSE.   Copy No. 9.
14/12/17.

1.   The Battalion will be relieved by the 10th Yorks Regt. in Front Line on night 15/16th December 1917, and become Bde. Reserve, going into quarters vacated by 10th Yorks Regt.
2.   Coys. will be relieved as follows,
"A" Coy. by 10th Yorks Regt. "B" Coy.   "C" Coy. by 10th Yorks Regt. "A" Coy.
"B" Coy. by 10th Yorks Regt. "D" Coy.   "D" Coy. by 10th Yorks Regt. "C" Coy.
3.   On completion of relief in Front Line and Supports, Coys. will take over places vacated by relieving units as follows,
"A" Coy. in Cavalry Trench   Coy. H.Q's W.18b92.
"B" Coy. in Brown Line   Coy. H.Q's W.18a9.3.
Bn. H.Q's. Coy. - C & D Coys. to S Side of Railway Embankment W.23.b.
4.   O.C. Coys. will send a report of work done in the Trenches during the Tour, to the Orderly Room by 2 p.m. 15th inst.
5.   Completion of relief will be reported to present Bn. H.Q's by Code word "HUNT", and arrival of A & B Coys. in their new positions by Code word "SWEET" to new Bn. H.Q's.
6.   O.C., A-C-D Coys. will detail 2 guides (1 per platoon) to report Bn. H.Q's at 4 p.m. to guide relieving Coys. to their quarters.
7.   O.C. Coys. will each detail an Advance party of 1 Officer - 1 N.C.O.- 2 Runners to report Bn. H.Q's at 10 a.m. to proceed and take over new quarters. The 2 Runners will thoroughly reconnoitre the routes in order to be able to guide Coys. on relief.
Advance parties from relieving Unit will arrive at Coys. H.Q's about 11 a.m.
8.   All Lewis Guns and Magazines will be carried by Coys. C & D Coys. will send any Officers Mess Canteens etc., to Bn. H.Q's by 2-30 p.m. sharp to be conveyed to new quarters.
Teas will be served at 3-30 p.m. sharp - and empty Dixies returned at once.
9.   All S.A.A., Rifle Grenades - S.O.S. Signals - Defence Schemes etc., will be handed over on relief.
10.   Acknowledge.

Sent by Runner at 7 p.m. 14/12/17.

Copy No. 1 Filed.
  "   " 2-6 Coys. & H.Q's Coy.
  "   " 7 62nd Infantry Bde.
  "   " 8 T.O. & Q.M.
  "   " 9 & 10 War Diary.

                                                                Captain & Adjutant.
                                                                     OXEN.

3/4th THE QUEEN'S R.W.S. REG.   OPERATION   Appendix 6
                                ORDER No. 31.
Map Ref. 57c S.E.   16/12/17   Copy No. 9.

1. The 62 Inf. Bde. will be relieved by the 64 I. Bde. in the left sector of Div. Front on the 17/18 Dec.
2. This Batt. will be relieved by 9th K.O.Y.L.I. as under.
   "A" Coy. by 9th KOYLI "D" Coy.
   "B" Coy.   Do.   "B" Coy.
   "C" Coy.   Do.   "C" Coy.
   "D" Coy.   Do.   "A" Coy.
   On completion of relief Coys. will move by Platoons to Railway Camp - HEUDICOURT.
3. All Grenades - R. Grenades - S.O.S.Sigs. - Defence Schemes etc., will be handed over on relief.
4. Completion of Relief will be reported to Present Bn. H.Qs by code word SKEET.
5. B & C Coys. will each send 2 guides (1 per platoon) to meet incoming Coys at BOX DUMP, W16 d.9.0. at 2 p.m.
6. Advance parties of 9th K.O.Y.L.I. will arrive at respective Coy.H.Q's at about 10.15 a.m.
7. O.C. Coys. will each send 1 off - 1 N.C.O. - 2 runners to report Bn. H.Q's at 9-15 a.m.. The runners will reconnoitre ground between present Coy. H.Q's and new camp and return to respective Coys. and act as guides to Coys. on relief.
7. Lewis Guns and Magazines will be carried by Coys.
   1 Limber will report A & B Coys. Cookhouse at 1.30 p.m. to convey
   Dixies, Coys. Canteens etc, to new camp.
Officers Mess Cart will report Bn. H.Q. at 1.30 p.m. to convey C & D Coys. Officers' Canteen to new camp.
Dinners will be served at 12.30 p.m.
Horses for Water Carts and Cooker will report at 1.30 p.m.
8. All huts etc., must be left thoroughly clean.
9. Transport and Nucleus will move under instructions already issued.
10. Acknowledge.

Issued by Runner at 8 p.m.
         16/12/17.

Copy No.1. Filed.   (Signed) V. F. Samuelson.
  - " 2-6 Coys.   Captain & Adjutant.
  - " 7 BOLT.   OXEN.
  - " 8 T.O. & Q.M.
  - " 9 & 10. War Diary.

Appendix 7

COPY OF REGIMENTAL ORDER, DATED 25th DECR, 1917.

No. 1686.- AWARD.

The following is an extract from Brigade Order No 15, d/24/12/17

"The Military Medal has been awarded to the following N. C. O.

No 201645, Sergt W. G. Ford, 3/4th "Queen's"(RWS)Regt.
("A" Company).

OPERATION ORDER, NO 33 by Appendix 8.
LT-COLONEL G. H. Sawyer, D.S.O., COMMANDING
3/4th Bn "The Queen's" (RWS) Regt.

Copy No 11

24. 12. 17

Ref Sheet 57 c S. E.

1. The 62nd Infantry Bde will relieve the 64th Inf Bde in the left Sector of the Div Front on the 26th inst.

2. This Battalion will relieve the 9th K O Y L I in the Centre-Sub Sector.

    "A" Coy will relieve "C" Coy 9th KOYLI in right Sector.
    "B" Coy -do- "A" Coy -do- left Sector
    "C" Coy -do- "D" Coy -do- right Support.
    "D" Coy -do- "B" Coy -do- left Support
    H.Q's Coy -do- H.Q's Coy -do- Batt H. Q's.

3. The Battalion will leave present Camp in following order, by platoons at 200 yards intervals, commencing at 4. 30 p.m.

    "B" Coy - "A" Coy - Bn H.Q's Coy - "C" Coy - "D" Coy.

4. 4 Lewis Guns and 64 Magazines per Coy will be carried by Coys. Rations for the 27th inst will be carried by Coys under instructio to be issued by Quartermaster.
The Coy Cooks will leave Camp at 2. 30 p.m. and report to Sergeant Lancester at New Bn H. Q's.
Teas will be issued in the line after completion of relief.

5. The Transport Officer will detail Officers' Mess Cart - and 2 Limbers - 1 Water Cart (full) to be at Bn H. Q's at 2.30 p.m., 26th inst, one to convey Coy Dixies, one to convey Coy's Canteens etc, which must be at Bn H. Q's by 2. 20 p.m. sharp.   Each Coy can send their Coy Cook and 1 Servant to accompany this limber and look after canteens etc.

6. Completion of relief will be reported to Bn H. Q's by code word "TRON".

7. Advance parties, as under, will leave Camp at 10 a.m.

    Each Coy - 1 Officer - 1. N.C.O - 2 Signallers - 1 Runner.

    H. Q's Coy - Sergt Harding, Sergt Lancester - 1 N.C.O - 2 Runners - 2 Signallers.

8. Camp must be left scrupulously clean and a Certificate to this effect sent to Bn H. Q's by 3 p.m.

9. All Grenades, S.A.A - S.O.S Signals,- Defence Schemes etc will be taken over on relief.

10. Acknowledge.

Issued by Orderly Sergeant 6 p.m. 24/12/17.

Copy No 1   Filed.
    2 - 6   Coys.
    7   9th K.O.Y.L.I.
    8   62nd Infantry Bde.
    9.   T.O.
    10.   Q.M.
    11.& 12   War Diary.

Captain & Adjutant,
3/4th Bn "The Queen's (RWS) Rgt

3/4th Bn "The Queen's" (RWS) Regt.

Order No 34.   Appendix G   Copy No

Secret.

Map Ref 57 c. S. E.

1. The Inter-Brigade Boundary will be changed to a line X 20.a.00.75 - X 19. b. 15. 30 - Railway at W. 24.d.3.4. on Dec 31st, 1917.

2. From above date (para 1) the 62nd Inf Bde will hold the left Sector of the Div's Front with two Battalions.
Inter Battalion boundary will be a line
X.14.a.o.2. - X. 13. Central - Railway X.13.c.2.9.

3. This Battalion will be relieved by 1st Lincolnshire Regt on the 31st inst. Relief will be commenced about 5 p.m.
On completion of relief this Battalion will move to Railway Camp - HEUDECOURT in Bde Reserve.

4. Completion of relief will be reported Bn H. Q's by Code Word "SWEET"

5. O. C. Coys will send a report of work done in the trenches and proposed work to Bn H. Q's by 1 p.m., 31st inst.

6. All movement E of RAILTON CROSS ROADS will be by platoons at 100 yds interval.

7. Lewis Guns and Magazines will be carried by Coys.
C & D Coys will carry the Blankets from Front line to Railway Camp and hand all over (25) to Q. M. next morning by 10 a.m.
Officers' Mess Canteens to be at Old Bde R. E. Dump (Nr Bn H.Q's) by 2.45 p.m. - 1 Officer's Servant and Coy Mess Cook can proceed from each Coy and accompany the Limber.
Teas will be served at 3.30 p.m. and Suppers will be served in Camp on arrival.

8. All Grenades - S.A.A. - S.O.S. Signals - Defence Schemes etc to be handed over on relief.

9. Advance Parties of 1 Officer - 1 N. C. O per Coy - except Bn H. Q's will leave present quarters at 9 a.m., 31st inst and proceed to Camp and report to Q. Master.

10. Transport & Nucleus will move under instructions already issued.

11. Acknowledge.

Issued by Runners   30. 12. 17.

Copy No 1   Filed.
     2-6   Coys.
     7   62nd Inf Bde.
     8.   M. C.
     9-10. War Diary.

Captain & Adjutant,
3/4th Bn "The Queen's"(RWS) Regt

WAR DIARY or INTELLIGENCE SUMMARY

Army Form C. 2118.

3/4th Bn Queens Royal Regt

January 1918

Place	Date	Hour	Summary of Events and Information	Remarks and references to Appendices
HEUDECOURT.	JANUARY 1.		Day spent in resting & cleaning up. Strength of Battalion 43 officers 757 O.R.	H.C.C.
do.	2		Day spent in kit inspections & bathing.	H.C.C.
do.	3		The C.O. reconnoitred the line preparatory to relief. Training continued	H.C.C.
do.	4		During the early morning the village, in the vicinity of the camp was subjected to a slight gas shell bombardment. The Battalion left billets at 4 p.m in order to relieve 1st Lincoln Regt in trenches around VAUCELETTE FARM, the relief was complete by 6.40 p.m. "A" Coy was on the right "B" Coy on the left in the front line whilst "C" Coy was in right support "D" Coy in left support in sunken road West of Battn H.Q. Hostile artillery intermittently active in vicinities of VAUCELETTE FARM, Battn H.Q. The Transport 10th Div. had moved service in the day to VILLARS FAUCON. Casualties NIL.	H.C.C. Appendices 1 " 2
Trenches around VAUCELETTE FARM & SAFFADUCOURT	5.		Quiet day. Hostile artillery inactive. During earlier part of the night the vicinities of VAUCELETTE FARM, Battn B H.Q. were bombarded by enemy field howitzers. Casualties O.R. 1 killed 2 wounded	H.C.C. Appendices 2
do.	6		Extremely quiet day & night. "C" Coy relieved "A" Coy on right of front line, relief complete at 7.07 p.m. Thaw set in. Casualties NIL.	H.C.C.
do.	7		Quiet day. Trenches, especially those on right, in very wet condition. The night passed without incident. Casualties NIL.	H.C.C.

WAR DIARY or INTELLIGENCE SUMMARY

Army Form C. 2118.

(Erase heading not required.)

Place	Date	Hour	Summary of Events and Information	Remarks and references to Appendices
Trenches around VAUCELETTE FARM S.of GOUZEAUCOURT	JANUARY 8		Hostile artillery fairly active during early part of morning on vicinity of VAUCELETTE FARM & Batt HQrs. The Batt was relieved by 1st Lancashire Regt during the evening, the relief being complete by 6.20 p.m. The Batt proceeded to dug-outs in new railway embankment S. East of HEUDECOURT, B Coy being accommodated in dug-outs in N.W. outskirts of PEZIERES. Quiet night. Casualties NIL.	W.C.C Appendix 2, 3
Railway Embankment East of HEUDECOURT	9		Working parties found for Tunnelling Companies R.E.	
do.	10.		Working parties found for R.E. The following officers joined the Battn :- 2nd Lts. J.T. Lancaster, R. Cheston, C.F. O'Shea, J.P. Phelps, J.E. Morton.	W.C.C.
do.	11		Working parties found for R.E.	W.C.C
do.	12		Working parties found for R.E. The Battalion left the Railway Embankment at 4.30 p.m. (proceeded to relieve the 1st Lincoln Regt in Trenches around) VAUCELETTE FARM. D Coy was on the right. C Coy on right support in CAVALRY SUPPORT TR., Railway cutting whilst 'A' Coy was on the right on the front line. 'B' Coy was in sunken road West of Batt HQs. The 10th Yorks Regt were on the left whilst 6th. Brigade were on the right. The relief was complete by 6.20 p.m. Hostile artillery was spasmodically active around Batt Hqrs during the evening. Trenches in very wet condition. Casualties O.R. 1 killed 4 wounded.	W.C.C Appendix 4, 2

WAR DIARY
INTELLIGENCE SUMMARY

Army Form C. 2118.

(Erase heading not required.)

Instructions regarding War Diaries and Intelligence Summaries are contained in F. S. Regs., Part II. and the Staff Manual respectively. Title pages will be prepared in manuscript.

Place	Date	Hour	Summary of Events and Information	Remarks and references to Appendices
Trenches around VAUCELETTE FARM S. of GOUZEAUCOURT	JANUARY 13		Hostile artillery substituted by active in vicinity of RACQUET TR & VAUCELETTE FARM during the afternoon. Patrol activity patrolled during the night. None of the enemy encountered. Casualties 1 O.R. wounded	W.C.C. Appendix 2
	14.		The enemy spasmodically shelled VAUCELETTE FARM, RACQUET TR & the "LOOP" during the day. John Coy. relief carried out during earlier part of the night. "A" & "D" Coy. in the front line being relieved by "C" & "B" Coy. respectively. "A" Coy. becoming Support Coy. & "D" Coy. going into Reserve. Casualties Nil.	W.C.C. Appendix 2
do.	15.		Intermittent enemy gun fire throughout the day. Casualties Nil. Patrol activity patrolled throughout the night. No enemy encountered.	W.C.C.
do.	16.		Hostile artillery active at intervals at VAUCELETTE FARM & the LOOP & the road near Batt.? H.Q. During the evening the Batt.? was relieved by 1st Lincolnshire Regt, the relief being complete by 7:10 p.m. The Batt.? proceeded into Brigade Reserve at HEUDICOURT from accommodation attached in huts N.W. of the village. Casualties O.R. 2 Killed 5 wounded	W.C.C. Appendix 2 " 5
HEUDICOURT	17.		Day spent in resting & cleaning up. Draft of 1/3 O.R. joined the Batt.?	W.C.C. W.C.C.
do	18.		Day spent in bathing & cleaning up.	W.C.C.
do	19.		Training commenced.	W.C.C.
do	20.		Took command of Anti-Aircraft defences of the Camp. The Batt.? relieved the 1st Lincolnshire Regt. in trenches around VAUCELETTE FARM, the 15th Yorkshire Regt. being on the left & 8th Warwickshire Regt. on the right. "A" & "D" Coys. were in the front line on the right & left respectively. "C" Coy. was in Support at railway. "D" Coy. was in reserve in sunken road & hurts front line of the Batt. HQ. whilst Batt. HQ. were accommodated in a new deep dug out in sunken road formerly the Batt.? Reserve Coy. Relief completed 7.25 p.m. Amount of Casualties Nil.	W.C.C. Appendix 6 " 2

WAR DIARY or INTELLIGENCE SUMMARY

(Army Form C. 2118.)

(Erase heading not required.)

Place	Date	Hour	Summary of Events and Information	Remarks and references to Appendices
Trenches around VAUCELETTE FARM S of GOUZEAUCOURT	JANUARY 21.		Quiet day. VAUCELETTE FARM shelled during the afternoon whilst No News kind was actively sniped during the night. None of the enemy were encountered. Casualties 1 O.R. wounded.	HCC
do.	22.		Hostile artillery active at intervals on VAUCELETTE FARM. Casualties 2 O.R. wounded. Relief by rly. Bde. C Coy. relieving D Coy. in front line respectively. A Coy. went into Support into Support. D Coy. went in reserve.	HCC Appendix ?
do.	23.		Quiet day. Enemy artillery intermittently active on left side of Battalion area during afternoon. Casualties 1 OR wounded.	HCC
do.	24.		Local shelling of VAUCELETTE FARM Vicinity. The Bn HQ was relieved by 12 Durham Light Inf. during the evening the relief being complete by 7.15 p.m. The Bn then proceeded into Brigade Reserve at the Railway Embankment East of HEUDICOURT. C Coy Coy accompanying attached on duty, each in N.W. outskirts of PEIZIERES.	HCC Appendix 2
Railway Embankment E. of HEUDICOURT	25.		Working parties found for R.E. Tunnelling Company. Day spent in resting.	HCC
do.	26.		Working parties found for R.E.	HCC
do.	27.		Working parties found for R.E. Officers & NCOs reconnoitred trenches preparing to relieve.	HCC
do.	28.		The Battalion left its billets to relieve the 1st Lancashire Regt in the trenches around VAUCELETTE FARM. A & D Coys were in front line on right respectively. C Coy was in Support 'B' Coy in reserve. the 16th Warwicks Regt was on the left on relief H.Q.N. Lincolnshire Regt was on the right. The relief commenced at 4.70.p.m. The enemy shelled the night & stood to Stanley & at stand-to, with 900 Casualties Nil.	HCC

Army Form C. 2118.

WAR DIARY
or
INTELLIGENCE SUMMARY.
(Erase heading not required.)

Instructions regarding War Diaries and Intelligence Summaries are contained in F. S. Regs., Part II. and the Staff Manual respectively. Title pages will be prepared in manuscript.

Place	Date	Hour	Summary of Events and Information	Remarks and references to Appendices
	JANUARY			
Trenches without HAVRINCOURT FARM SW of GOUZEAUCOURT	29		Very quiet day. Advanced Posts in of 17th Sherwood Foresters arrived p/ wanting to relieve Quiet night. Casualties O.R. 1 wounded (accidentally)	H.C.C
do	30		Spasmodic shelling of vicinity of HAVRINCOURT FARM during the morning. Relief was relieved by the 17th Sherwood Foresters 117th Brigade 39th Division during the morning. The relief being complete by 8.10 p.m. The Battalion was escorted by the Divisional Railway from HEUDICOURT to MOISLAINS, WK of PERONNE & accommodated in huts to the East of the village. The transport & horse-transport 5mm. moving by road from VILLERS FAUCON. The move was entirely completed by 12 noon. Casualties Nil.	H.C.C Appendix in 9
MOISLAINS	31		Day spent in resting, cleaning up.	H.C.C

E.H.Hoare Ltd Col
Commanding the Battn. The Queens Regt.

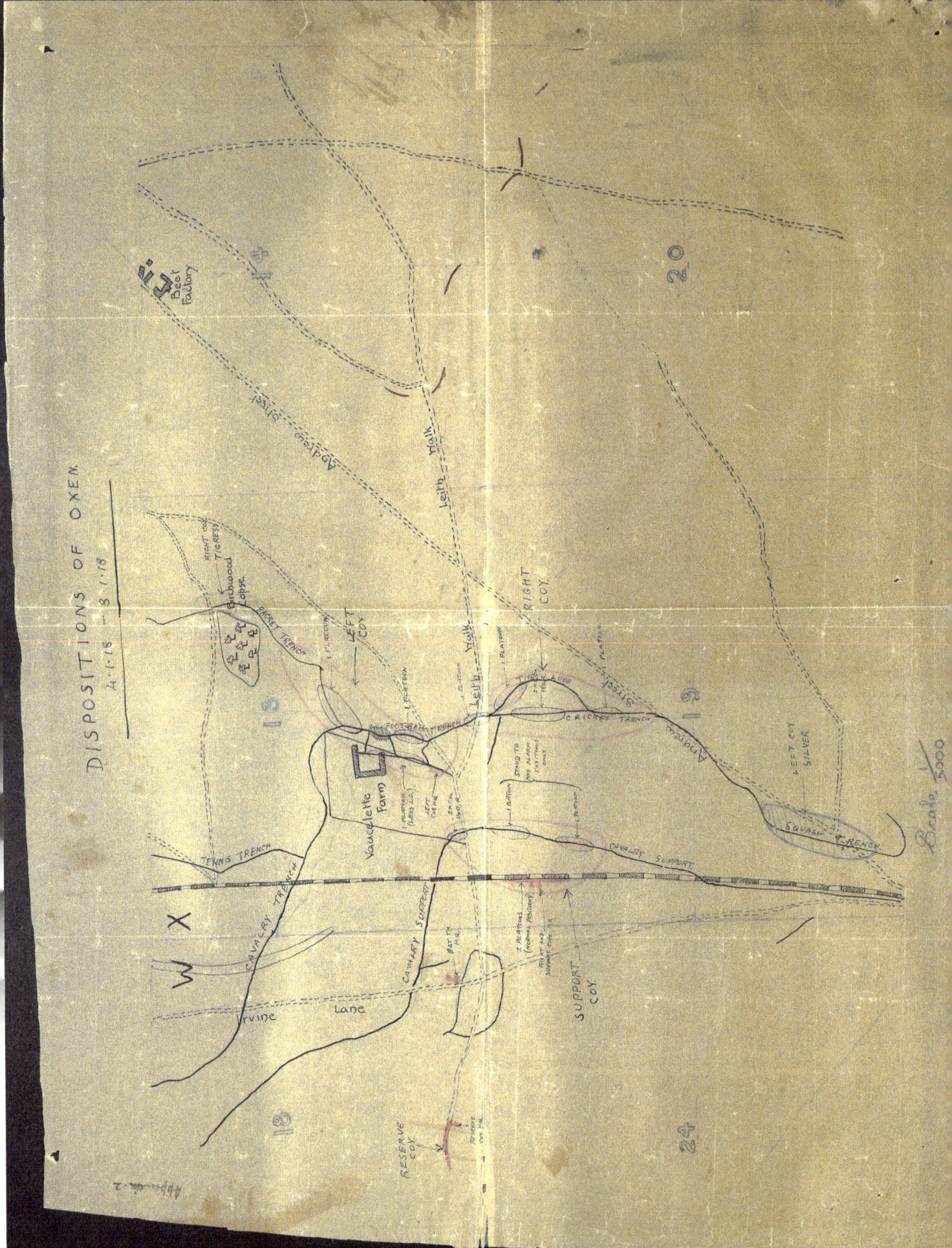

3/4th Bn "The Queen's" (RWS) Regt.   Appendix

Order No 35.   Copy No 12

SECRET.

Map Ref 57.c.S.E.   3.1.18.

1. This Battalion will relieve the 1st Lincoln Regt in the right Sub-Sector on the 4th inst.

2. Companies will take over as follows :-

    "A" Coy from 1st Lincoln's   "C" Coy - Right Front.
    "B"   -do-   "B" " - Left Front.
    "C"   -do-   "D" " - Support (Brown Line)
    "D"   -do-   "A" " - Reserve (Near Bn H. Q's)
    Bn H.Q's Coy -do-   Bn H. Q's Coy

3. The Battalion will leave Camp in following order, first platoon leaving at 4 p.m. and remainder at 200 yds interval.

    "A" Coy - "B" Coy - H. Q's Coy - "C" Coy - "D" Coy

4. Teas will be issued in Trenches after Relief complete.
    Rations for the 5th will be carried by the men under instructions to be issued by the Quartermaster.
    "A" & "B" Coys will each carry 25 Blankets for Front Line Shelters, and redraw from Q. M. after tour.
    Lewis Guns & Magazines (16 per gun) will be carried as before.

5. Transport Officer will detail Officers' Mess Cart and two Limbers to be at Bn H. Q's at 2.30 p.m. One Limber to convey dixies etc - one to convey Company Officers Canteens which must be at Bn H. Q's by 2.15 p.m. sharp. Coy Cook and one Officer's servant can accompany the Limber.

6. Advance Party consisting of 1 Officer, 1 N. C. O, 1 Coy Runner, 2 Signallers per Coy including H. Q's Coy will leave Camp at 9.30 a.m. to proceed to Front Line and take over Stores etc.

7. Relief complete will be reported to New Bn H. Q's by Code Word "SNAP".

8. All Ranks not proceeding to Front Line will parade at Bn H. Q's at 2.15 p.m. to proceed to Transport Lines.

9. Officers' Valises and all Blankets, clearly labelled by Coys in team will be handed Q. M. Stores by 12 noon.
    Officers' Valises & Blankets of men proceeding to Transport Lines will be handed to Q. M. Stores by 9 a.m..

10. All Trench Stores, Defence Schemes etc will be taken over on relief.

11. Acknowledge.

    Issued by Runners   p.m. 3/1/18.

    Copy No 1   Filed.
         2-6   Coys.
         7.   62nd Inf Bde H. Q's
         8.   Q. M.
         9.   T. O.
         10.   1st Lincoln Regt.
         11 & 12. War Diary.

                                    Captain & Adjutant,
                                    3/4th Bn "The Queen's" (RWS) Regt

3/4th Bn "The Queen's" (RWS) Regt.

Operation Order No 35.

Appendix 3

Copy No. 9

Ref Sheet 57 c S. E.   7. 1. 18.

1. The Battalion will be relieved in the Right Sub-Sector by the 1st Lincolnshire Regt on the 8th inst.
   The Battalion will move to Railway Embankment in Bde Support, and take over from 12/13th Northumberland Fusiliers.

2. Coys will take over quarters from 12/13th North: Fusiliers, as under.

   "A" Coy from North: Fusiliers "A" Coy.
   "B"   -do-   "C" "   (PEZIERES)
   "C"   -do-   "B" "
   "D"   -do-   "D" "
   H.Q's Coy -do-   H.Q's Coy.

3. Midday meal will be served at 12.30 p.m., 8th inst and Teas 3.30 p.m. There will be Hot Tea ready at Embankment on arrival.

4. Coy Officers' Canteens will be sent to H. Q's Coy Cookhouse by 2 p.m. and 1 Servant & Coy Cook can accompany them.

5. Lewis Guns - Magazines (25) Blankets will B carried.

6. A report of work done and proposed work will be sent Bn H. Q's by 12 noon.

7. Advance parties of 1 Off - 1 N. C. O - 2 Runners per Coy will report H. Q's North: Fusiliers at 2 p.m. to take over Lines and remain, except the two Runners who will reconnoitre the route thoroughly returning to Coys to act as guides.

8. Completion of Relief will be reported by Runner to these H. Q's by Code Word "CRASH" and arrival at Railway Embankment by code word "COLES".

9. All S. A A - S. O. S. Signals - Defence Schemes etc will be handed over on relief.

10. Acknowledge.

Issued by Runner 9 p.m. 7/1/18.

Copy No 1 Filed.
    ,,   2-6 Coys.
          7   62nd Infy Bde.
          8 & 9 War Diary.

V. F. Samuelson

Captain & Adjutant,
3/4th Bn "The Queen's"(RWS)Regt

Appendix 4
Copy No. 11.

Secret

3/4th Bn "The Queen's" (R.W.S.) Regt.
Battalion Order No. 24.

11.1.18

Ref. Map 57 c N.E.

1. This Battalion will relieve the 1st Lincoln Regt in the Right Sub Sector on 12th Jan, 1918.

2. Allotment will be as under.

   "A" Coy   Right Sub Sector.   Front Line.
   "B" "   Battn Reserve.
   "C" "   Battn Support.
   "D" "   Left Sub Sector.   Front Line.

   The Battalion will leave present quarters, commencing at 4.30 p.m. in following order by Platoons at 100 yards interval.

   "D" Coy - "A" Coy - H.Q's Coy - "C" Coy - "B" Coy.

3. Advance Parties of 1 Officer - 1 N.C.O. - 2 Signallers - 1 Runner per Coy, will report H. Q's 1st Lincolnshire Regt at 2.15 p.m. 12th Inst.

4. All S. A. A. - T. M. Signals - Mo Guards etc will be taken over on relief.

5. Completion of Relief will be reported few in H. Q's by code word "WILLIE".

6. Administrative Orders issued.

7. The present camp will be taken over by 1st Lincolnshire Regt.

8. Huts will be left scrupulously clean, and a certificate to this effect sent in H. Q's by 2.30 p.m.

9. Acknowledge.

Issued by Runner at 6 p.m. 11.1.18.

Copy No 1 Filed.
       2-6 Coys.
       7 82nd Infty Bde.
       8 1st Lincolnshire Regt.
       9 Q.M. & T.O.
       10 & 11 Filed.

V.F. Samuelson

Captain & Adjutant,
3/4th Bn. "The Queen's"(R.W.S.)Regt.

Appendix 5

3/4th Bn "The Queen's" (R.W.S.) Regt.

Operation Order No 38.

SECRET.   Jan 15th, 1916.

Relief of Bn in T.L.

1. The 3/4th "Queen's" will be relieved by the 1st Lincolnshire Regt. on Jany 16th.

2. On relief the Battn will proceed to SAILLCOURT & become Bde Reserve.

3. All Trench Stores, Maps, Defence Schemes, Scoops, &c. on Dump Guard will be handed over on relief.

4. O. C. Coys will render a report of work done during tour in the trenches & also proposed programme of work to these H. Q's by 8 p.m., 16.1.16.

5. On Jany 16th, Dinners will be served at 12.30 p.m. and Teas at 3. 30 p.m.

6. Officers' Mess Canteen, accompanied by 1 Cook & 1 Servant, will be at S. H. Q's at 2.15 p.m.

7. An advance party of 1 Officer, 1 N. C. O and 1 Runner will report to Capt W. F. Dennison, M. C at 11 a.m., Jany 16th at RAILWAY CAMP.

8. Completion of relief will be reported to these H. Q's by code word "ERNST".

9. Acknowledge.

Issued by Runner at 4.30 p.m. 15/1/16.

Copy No 1 Filed.
  2-6 Coys.
  7 62nd Inf Bde.
  8. 1st Lincoln Regt
  9 & 10 War Diary.

                                               Lieut,
                                          For Adjutant,
                                               QUEEN.

Appendix 6

Appx No 12.

2/4th Bn The Queen's (R.W.S.) Regt

OPERATION ORDER No. 19.

By...

Ref. Map &c.

1. The Battalion will relieve the 1st Lincolnshire Regt in the Right Sub-Sector on the 20th inst.

2. The Battalion will leave present camp in following order by Platoons at 100 yds interval, commencing at 4.30 p.m.
   "C" Coy - "A" Coy - H.Q. "B" Coy - "D" Coy - "E" Coy.

3. All Stores - Tools - Bombs - Defence Schemes - Code Cards &c will be taken over in situ.

4. Relief complete will be reported to Bde H.Q.'s by Code Word "CHERRY".
   (Coy Canteens etc. under arrangements will be at Bde carts but by 3 p.m.)

5. (Lewis Guns and Rifles will be inspected.
   (Coys will carry nothing extra, blankets under own arrangements.

6. All blankets, each in bundles of ten and labelled, will be ready by 8 a.m. to be returned.
   All kitbags - each to be labelled at Bn Qmst's hut ready for loading at 3 p.m.
   Officers' Valises - in company bundles at their huts by 12 noon to be collected.
   Teas will be issued before relief is complete.
   Each man will be issued with 1 pair of dry socks to be taken to the trenches.

7. All reinforcements for Transport Lines will report Bn H.Q.'s at 2 p.m. ready to move.

8. Coys will take over as follows :-
   "B" Coy from "Castle's" "C" Coy - Right Front.
   "   "   -do-   -do-   "A" "   - Reserve.
   "   "   -do-   -do-   "D" "   - Support.
   "   "   -do-   -do-   "B" "   - Left Front.
   "   " Coy -do-   -do-   H.Q.

9. All men who Company considers unfit for the Trenches will report M.O. at Sick Parade 8.30 a.m. and be marked "Trenches" or otherwise.

10. Advance Party of 1 Officer - 1 N.C.O - 1 Signaller - 1 Runner per Coy will leave Camp at 2 p.m.

11. Mens' Surplus Kits will be dumped at R.Q.M. Sgt's Hut by 11 a.m. - 5 men to 1 sandbag - Sandbags must be clearly labelled with names.

12. Bn H.Q's will be in Sunken Road W. 18. c.
    Reserve Coys are accommodated in Old Bn H.Q's lines.

13. Acknowledge.

Issued by Runner at   Pres. 19.1.18.

Copy No 1 Filed.
       2-6 Coys.
         7 Cmd. 1st Bde.
         8 1st Lincolnshire Regt.
         9 T. O. & S.
        10 Bde. Major.
     11 & 12 War Diary.

V. Hamilton
Captain & Adjutant,
2/4th Bn "The Queen's"(R.W.S)
Regt.

The following ... ...

Para 2. ... ... 30 pts.

Para 6. ... ... will be issued after relief is completed
... ... will be served in camp at 4 p.m.

Line - ... ... to be a bachelor's hat etc. - cross a ped
... ... 30 pts.

Para 7. Add - ... ...

Officers ... ... to the ... III Corps School will proceed to
Transport Lines.

Issued to all in receipt of above orders.

Capt. & Adjutant,
...

SECRET.   3/4th Bn "The Queen's" (RWS) Regt.   Copy No 12.
           OPERATION ORDERS NO. 40.   Appendix
                                                 23. 1. 18

Map Ref 57 c S. E.

1. The Battalion will be relieved in the right Subsector by the
   1st Lincolnshire Regt at about 6. 30 p.m., the 24th inst.
   The Battalion will proceed to Railway Embankment in Brigade Support.
   Coys will take over from Corresponding Coys of Northumberland
   Fusiliers.
   "C" Coy will be at FEZIRANG and O. C. "C" Coy will make out a scheme
   for the action of this Coy in case of attack.

2. Advance parties of 1 Officer - 1 N. C. O and 1 Runner per Coy will
   report O.C's Northumberlands at 2 p.m. to take over.

3. Relief complete will be reported these H. Q's by Code Word "BOLO".

4. All S. O. S Signals - Defence Schemes, SOS Boards etc will be
   handed over on relief.

5. Midday meal will be served at 12. 30 p.m. - Tea 4 p.m.
   Soup will be served on arrival at Camp.

6. Transport Officer to have one Limber at "A" - "B" - "C" Coys
   cookhouse to pick up Dixies and return via "D" Coy & Bn. H. Q's
   cookhouse to pick up those Dixies and take them to Embankment.
   1 Limber to report at "A" - "B" - "C" Coys Cookhouse at 4. 45 p.m.
   and return via "D" Coy H. Q's and pick up Coy Canteens etc.
   Coy Cook and 1 Officer's Servant per Coy to accompany this Limber.
   Officers' Mess Cart to be at H. Q's at 4. 45 p.m.

7. Acknowledge.

   Issued by Runner at   p.m. 23/1/18.

   Copy No1   Filed.
        2-6 Coys.
        7.   62nd Infy Bde.
        8.   T. O & M. O.
        9.   1st Lincoln Regt.
        10.   Reg Sergt Major.
        11 & 12 War Diary.

                                              V. Hamilton
                                              Captain & Adjutant,
                                              3/4th Bn "The Queen's"(RWS)
                                                              Regt.

5/4th Bn "The Queen's" (R.W.S.) Regt.

Appendix 8

Copy No **11.**

OPERATION ORDER No 41.

Jany 27th, 1918.

SECRET.

No 1 of 57 & R.E.

1. The Battalion will relieve the 1st Lincolnshire Regt in the right sub-sector on Jany 28th.

2. Coys will start at 5.30 p.m. and move by platoons at 100 yards intervals in the following order :-

    "B" Co to Left Front Sector.
    "A" Co   Right   "
    "C" Co   Reserve
    "D" Co   Support
    "E" Co   Reserve.

3. All Lamps, Brigade Guards etc to be taken over on relief.
   Gum boots will not be taken into the line this time.

4. An advance party of 1 Officer - 1 N.C.O. & 1 Signaller and 1 runner per Co will report to 1st Lincolnshire Regt by 2 p.m.

5. Rations for Jany 29th will be carried by Coys on usual arrangements.

6. Teas on Jany 28th will be served in present camp at 4 p.m.

7. All Coy Cartoons (accompanied by 1 Cook & 1 Servant) & Dixies to be at these H.Q's by 8.00 p.m. for to-night.

8. All Blankets rolled in bundles of 10 & clearly labelled & Officers valises to be ready for loading by 11 a.m.
   Position of Dump to be notified later.

9. Completion of relief to be reported these H.Q's by Coys Cmdr T.O.C.A.

10. Acknowledge.

Copies to Coys etc.

Copy No 1 Allot.
    2-5 Coys.
     "   1st Lincoln's Regt.
     "   68rd Inf. Bde.
     "
    10 & 11 War Diary.

J. Samuelson
Lieut & Adjutant,
5/4th Bn "The Queen's"
(R.W.S.)Regt

Appendix 8

3/4th Bn "The Queen's" (RWS) Regt.

OPERATION ORDER NO 42.

Appendix
Copy No 10

SECRET.

Map Ref 57 c S. E.
         62 c

30. 1. 18.

1. The 117th Inf Bde will relieve the 62nd Inf Bde in the left Sector of Divisional Front on Jan 30th.

2. The 17th Sherwood Foresters will relieve this Battalion in the right Subsector as under :-

   "A" Coy will be relieved by "C" Coy Sherwood Foresters.
   "B" Coy   -do-   "A" Coy   -do-
   "C" Coy   -do-   "D" Coy   -do-
   "D" Coy   -do-   "B" Coy   -do-
   Bn H. Q's Coy   -do-   Bn H. Q's Coy   -do-

3. Programmes of work done and suggested will be handed over and a Copy sent to Bn H. Q's by 3 p.m., 30th inst.
   All Defence Schemes - Maps - Aeroplane Photos - Grenades - S.O.S Signals etc and all documents relating to the Sector will be handed over on relief.
   A nominal roll of all trench stores to be handed over will be sent Orderly Room by 3 p.m., 30th inst.

4. Completion of Relief will be sent Bn H. Q's Coy by Code Word "SAM".

5. The Battalion will move by train to Camp "E" MOISLAINS" (62 c C.18. C.6.8. approx) on completion of relief as under.
   Coys will move by platoons at 100 yds interval and proceed to entraining place (sheet 57 c S. E. W.14.b.1.9).
   The Company Commander will report all present to the entraining Officer, Capt J.LOCKIE, M. C. 12/13th Northumberland Fusiliers, who will give instructions re entraining.

6. Lewis Guns and Magazines will be carried by Coys.
   Coy Commanders will make their own arrangements re having Canteens etc sent to X Roads W.15.d.95.60 (Sheet 57c S. E.) by 5.45 p.m., where they will be handed over to L/Corp SWEETMAN.
   One man per Coy will be left in charge of these Stores which will be conveyed by Lorry.
   All dixies will be sent X Roads W.18.d.8.1 between 5 and 5.15 p.m. and be carried to X Roads W.15.d.95.60 by a fatigue party to be found by "B" Coy.
   (N. B. Not more than 1 man per Coy is to travel on the Lorry).

7. O. C. Coys will each detail 1 guide per Platoon (4 per Coy) to be at Road Junction about W.18.C.3.2.(Western end of Sunken Road) at 5. 30 p.m. to guide relieving platoons to positions.
   These guides will report at above point to 2/Lieut STEVENSON who will be responsible that the guides meet their right platoons.

8. Lieut A. E. FROST, M. C and 1 N. C.O from "B" Coy will report to Staff Captain, 62nd Infantry Bde at 3 p.m. to-day to receive instructions as to entraining point.
   The N. C. O will after reconnoitring the entraining point, be sent to X Roads W.15.d.95.60. where he will remain and direct each platoon when it arrives there as to the route to be taken.
   Lieut A. E. FROST, M. C. will meet each platoon on arrival at entraining point and issue any instructions he may have received.

9. The Battalion will detrain at D. 20.d (Sheet 62 c) where guides will meet Coys and take them direct to Camp. Approx C.18.C (Sheet 62c)

P.T.O

10. Coy Commanders will report by Runner to New Bn H.Q's when their Coys are in Camp.

11.) Acknowledge.

Issued by Runner at 11.15 a.m. 30.1.18

Copy No 1 Filed.
     2-6 Coys.
       7 62nd Inf Bde.
       8 17th Sherwood Foresters.
     9 & 10 War Diary.

                                        Captain & Adjutant,
                                3/4th Bn "The Queen's"(RWS) Regt.

ADDITION TO B. O. ORDER NO 42.

Ref para 7, after :- that the guides meet their right platoons, add:-

Each man must be given written instructions stating Coy. and No. of Platoon he has to guide.

Issued to all in receipt of B.O. 42.

                                        Captain & Adjutant,
                                3/4th Bn "The Queen's"(RWS)Regt.

30.1.18

www.ingramcontent.com/pod-product-compliance
Lightning Source LLC
Chambersburg PA
CBHW081533160426
43191CB00011B/1753